Research Concepts for the Practitioner of Educational Leadership

Research Concepts for the Practitioner of Educational Leadership

By

Lee Baldwin

BRILL
SENSE

LEIDEN | BOSTON

All chapters in this book have undergone peer review.

The Library of Congress Cataloging-in-Publication Data is available online at http://catalog.loc.gov

Typeface for the Latin, Greek, and Cyrillic scripts: "Brill". See and download: brill.com/brill-typeface.

ISBN 978-90-04-36513-1 (paperback)
ISBN 978-90-04-36511-7 (hardback)
ISBN 978-90-04-36515-5 (e-book)

Copyright 2018 by Koninklijke Brill NV, Leiden, The Netherlands.
Koninklijke Brill NV incorporates the imprints Brill, Brill Hes & De Graaf, Brill Nijhoff, Brill Rodopi, Brill Sense and Hotei Publishing.
All rights reserved. No part of this publication may be reproduced, translated, stored in a retrieval system, or transmitted in any form or by any means, electronic, mechanical, photocopying, recording or otherwise, without prior written permission from the publisher.
Authorization to photocopy items for internal or personal use is granted by Koninklijke Brill NV provided that the appropriate fees are paid directly to The Copyright Clearance Center, 222 Rosewood Drive, Suite 910, Danvers, MA 01923, USA. Fees are subject to change.

This book is printed on acid-free paper and produced in a sustainable manner.

Contents

1 Introduction   1

2 Overview of Research   3
   1   How Do We Know What We Know?   3
   2   What Are the Categories of Research?   5
   3   Overview of the Research Process   7

3 Beginning the Research Project
Topic, Problem Statement, Purpose Statement, and Research Questions   9
   1   Developing the Topic   9
   2   The Problem Statement   10
   3   The Purpose Statement   10
   4   Research Questions   11
   5   Definition of Terms   11

4 Finding and Reviewing Literature for Credible Research   13

5 Populations and Samples   15
   1   Identifying the Population   15
   2   Obtaining the Population   16
   3   Types of Random Samples   17
   4   Non-Random Sampling   20
   5   Sample Size   21

6 Measurement of Variables   23

7 Internal and External Validity and Threats to Validity   31
   1   Threats to Internal Validity   31

8 Research Designs and Their Limitations   37
   1   Experimental Research Designs   37
   2   Correlational Research   41
   3   Causal-Comparative Research   41
   4   Survey Research   43
   5   Action Research   46
   6   Single Subject Designs   47

9 **Qualitative Research**   49
  1   Types of Purposive Sampling   51
  2   Validity in Analyzing Data   52
  3   Combining Methods and Mixed-Methods Research Designs   53

10 **Analysis of Data**   55
  1   Categories of Data   55
  2   Types of Data Analysis   56

11 **Research Results**
  Conclusions, Decisions, and Actions   60
  1   Sections of a Research Report   60
  2   Writing the Research Report   63
  3   Presenting Results of a Research Study   65
  4   Key Factors in Presenting Research   66

Further Reading   69

Index   70

CHAPTER 1

Introduction

Welcome to the world of research in education! This monograph is designed to acquaint you with the basic principles of educational research that are most applicable to today's educational leader. There are increasing demands on the school based educational leaders as well as those in educational leadership at other levels such as school districts, state agencies, foundations and other areas. While this monograph is primarily focused on using and applying research at the school level, the ideas presented are applicable in many different areas as well.

When we think of the demands on educational leaders today, it doesn't take long to realize that there are ever-increasing demands on the principal and other school leaders. Previously, perhaps 20 years ago, a principal could run a school very successfully by being a good manager. A good manager would be sure the school was organized, ran smoothly and conflicts were minimized. With the advent of school effectiveness research that showed the relationships between student achievement and school factors and the arrival of school accountability, new demands were placed on educational leaders. These demands were added to and did not replace the demands on principals to be good managers. These demands not only added to the workload but also introduced wholly new knowledge and skills needed by principals to be successful.

The new knowledge and skills that are presently needed and varied but can be summarized as being primarily moving the principal from being a manager to a leader, especially an instructional leader. The requirement of a principal to be an instructional leader has meant having a deep understanding of curriculum and instruction. This knowledge has always been desirable but now has become essential. Today the principal needs to be able to work with teachers to improve instruction, consult with parents on what students are expected to know and understand, and work with committees such as professional learning communities to foster better instruction.

The advent of standardized testing with accountability requirements has brought another domain to what the instructional leader needs to develop expertise. A quick glance at test results is not sufficient for ensuring that the school is a highly functional school where students are learning. Today's principal needs to be skilled at analyzing standardized test data and other data to develop a sense of the state of the school. This analysis includes identifying strengths and weaknesses of the results, determining which differences are significant and require action, and developing intervention plans to address weaknesses found.

At the same time as testing has proliferated, the amount of data available to the school leader has multiplied exponentially. Data bases today are much more comprehensive and accessible, leading to large amounts of data available to the school leader. The availability of data provides opportunities not previously possible to use data, but also requires skills in the use of data not previously required. With the availability of standardized test data, other data, and the availability of data systems, there is a much greater opportunity and necessity to be able to analyse data for making decisions on improvements in schools. Data-based decision making means being able to use data effectively to make sound decisions as an instructional leader.

The overall purpose of this monograph is to help the future or current educational leader to use research and data analysis skills to make better decisions as an instructional leader. Specific purposes will be as follows:

- Understanding the role of educational research for the educational leader
- Using research principles to promote instructional leadership through data-based decision making
- Introduction to research principles to critique research
- Introduction to understanding how to analyze data to make appropriate conclusions

Hopefully, this text will help you understand and be able to apply principles of research in your career as an educational leader. The principles of research discussed in this monograph focus on the practical needs that principals and other educational leaders have to access and critique information available on best practices in education and to use the best techniques to analyze data appropriately so that it produces valid and useful information that can be used in making decisions.

CHAPTER 2

Overview of Research

What is research? Research has been defined in numerous ways. But basically, research is an organized process of gathering and analyzing data to gain better understandings of the world around us. This process can help us grow in our knowledge and understanding of the world. Although research can play a major role in our knowledge and understanding of our world, not everything we know is based on research.

1   How Do We Know What We Know?

There are several ways in which we learn or know things about our world. Each way of knowing has its advantages and disadvantages. One way is through sensory experiences. A sensory experience is something that we perceive through our senses. It can be as basic as touching a hot stove and realizing that the action can cause a painful burn. We learn from that experience to not touch a hot oven again. We may also go to a concert and either find it interesting or boring. How we perceive the concert, will affect our conclusions about it and our decisions about attending another similar concert. Sensory experiences are a valuable source of our knowledge, but we are not able to personally experience everything in life.

A second way in which we learn is through experience. This experience is a bit higher level that just sensing something, but still is based on what we learn and perceive through our life experiences. This experience can be in our personal lives or in our professional lives. As a professional, we learn from our experiences, gaining knowledge and understandings about how things work in our lives. Most people who have been teachers will say that the first year is the hardest. The main reason that it is hard is that at the beginning, we do not have any professional experience to fall back on. The second year is usually easier because we have gained experience that we can rely on. The value of experience applies to almost everything we do regularly. The main disadvantage of experience is that we are limited by what we have experienced, and that may close our eyes to other ways to do things. Maybe we never thought of that in our experience or maybe we had a bad experience, but that was an exception.

A third way of gaining knowledge is through agreement with others. By communicating with others, we learn for the experience of others. This collaboration helps to broaden our knowledge and can take advantage of the wisdom of the group, which is usually more reliable than just the knowledge of one person. We can learn from others and broaden our scope of experiences. A disadvantage of relying on the consensus of others is that the others may be wrong or limited in their knowledge. Maybe everyone in the group thinks alike and has the same viewpoints. If this is the case, knowledge is limited and mistakes are made. A majority on a committee may not come to be best conclusion. Maybe people around you are set in their ways and not open to new ideas. There are many examples in history of making mistakes because a small group had limited perspective or knowledge.

A fourth way of knowing is through expert opinion. We cannot be expert in everything, so we get information from people who have much experience in an area or are specialized in that area. They can add wisdom and insight that we will not be able to match. However, experts can also be wrong. They may also be experts in general, but their expertise may not fit a specific situation.

A fifth way of knowing is through logical reasoning. We think that a certain action taken in a previous situation led to a good result. Logically when confronted with a similar situation, we think the same action may get the same result. Fundamentally, we may reason that if A equals B and B equals C, then A must equal C. This is a logical conclusion. It assumes that the first two parts, the premise, are true. If it turns out that they are not true under all conditions we make a logical error. The first situation may differ from the second situation in ways we do not expect.

The sixth and final way of knowing something is through the scientific method. The scientific method is the basis for scientific investigations. It is used in the physical sciences as well as in the social sciences, including education. The method is based on developing a question or hypothesis and then testing it under controlled conditions. We draw conclusions from the results of the testing, and this process adds to our knowledge.

The scientific method is a rigorous procedure that is followed in research studies. Specific details vary across different disciplines and situations, but the fundamental method is the basis of research today. First, the researcher states and defines the problem. Second, a hypothesis or research question is developed. Next, the researcher determines what information needs to be collected to answer the question and collects the information or conducts the research. Once the information is collected, the information is analyzed and organized. Finally, the researcher interprets the information and draws conclusions from the data collected.

All of the ways I that we know things have advantages, and we discover new things through all of the methods. Each has its advantages and disadvantages. The scientific method is the most rigorous and, if done correctly and objectively, is the most powerful way to build knowledge. As an educational leader you do not have the luxury of conducting a formal study every time a decision needs to be made. We often make decisions based on our experience, a consensus of a team, or the expertise of others. However, if we are confronted with a major problem to solve and we have the time to analyze the problem methodically, the scientific method is the best method to form the basis for gaining the best knowledge to solve the problem.

2   What Are the Categories of Research?

Research is a broad term and is conducted for many reasons or purposes. Not all of the purposes are directly applicable to the practitioner. Basic research attempts to develop basic understandings of the phenomena studied. Results may not be immediately useful and ultimately are used to build general conclusions and theory. The goal of basic research is to publish the research in scholarly journals which then contributes to the basic understandings of the topic. Applied research examines the effectiveness of practices. The main goal of applied research is to improve practice. Results are often published, but usually in publications that focus on the applications of research to practice. In education, applications research is often published in professional conferences and application oriented literature. Applications research also includes evaluation studies of a specific program. A third type of research is action research. Action research is a more informal type of research carried out by practitioners to systematically collect information, analyze it, and make decisions to improve practice. Since this is an informal type of research, it is often carried out by practitioners who do not have much formal training in research. The biggest value of action research is that it provides direct information to improve practice. Although all three categories of research describe here are important, basic research is seldom conducted by the school practitioner or educational leader. Although basic research is very valuable about understanding the theories and basic principles of education, the great majority of any research done be the school practitioner, will fall into the category of applications research or action research. Thus, this monograph will focus on these two categories of research.

Another way to distinguish research is by the type of research conducted. Traditionally research has adopted the scientific method and has focused on collecting quantitative data, which is then analyzed using appropriate statistical procedures and then drawing conclusions from the findings.

Within the framework of quantitative research, several types of research are found. Survey or descriptive studies usually collect a large amount of data and then draw conclusions that describe the population being studied. We are all familiar with surveys and public opinion polls. Survey research is an efficient way of gathering a large amount of data and then making generalizations that describe a population. Opinion polls that tell how people plan to vote in an upcoming election are constantly in the news before elections and are good examples of survey research.

Correlational research is a type of research which goes beyond just describing a population. In correlational research data are collected and relationships between and among variables are explored. Causal-comparative studies are often used in research studies where the purpose is to examine possible cause and effect relationships. In these research studies it would be impractical, unethical, or impossible to conduct an experiment so procedures are used to try to identify causes of outcomes when the groups have already been formed. As an example we might want to know if early childhood literacy experiences have an effect on reading comprehension in elementary school. It would probably be impossible or at least unethical to conduct an experiment where we randomly assign students to two groups where one group gets early childhood education and the other group is denied the experience. However, this research can be very valuable in understanding the factors that may lead to some outcome, either positive or negative.

Finally there is experimental research. This type of research is often called the gold standard of research. This is research that we often think of as the scientist in a laboratory conducting and experiment under very carefully controlled conditions. This same type of research can also be used in the social sciences but is difficult to conduct outside of a laboratory environment.

Another major type of research is qualitative research. Qualitative research has gotten an impetus in recent years as a reaction to or against the traditional research types described above. Qualitative research can range along a continuum from taking a totally different approach to research to a traditional approach to research with a greater reliance on qualitative data instead of quantitative data. Qualitative research includes include several types of research. Narrative studies describe in rich detail events that are observed. A second type of qualitative research is called ethnographic studies. In this type of study, the researcher embeds himself or herself in a situation and tries to understand and record the culture in which he or she is embedded. A third type of research is the case study. A case study is a detailed description of a single case, situation, or event. It may be an individual, a classroom or a program.

3   Overview of the Research Process

A research project is an organized sequential process of defining the scope of the project, determining the methods used to conduct the project, analyzing the data collected, and reporting the results. This sequence of events follows very closely the scientific method. The following section provides a descriptive overview of the specific steps in carrying out research project. Sometimes inexperienced researchers start collecting data without a clear plan on what data are needed or what the purpose of the project is. This usually leads to frustrations of lacking key data or not adequately answering the key questions.

First we need to clearly understand what the problem is that we are studying. What need are we trying to meet by conducting research? Without a clear need, we have many other things to do. This process results in a problem statement, which is a description of the background and rationale for the study. Why is the topic important to research? If we cannot express a clear answer to this question, we probably have better things to do with limited time.

Once we have clarified the problem statement and we clearly understand the need for research, we need to define the purpose of what we hope to accomplish by conducting the research. The purpose statement is a short statement of what is to be accomplished in the study.

Research questions are then developed that guide and focus the study on specific questions that will be answered in the study. The study seeks to answer the questions. Most research in education uses research questions to guide the study. Sometimes a research hypothesis is used instead of or in addition to the research questions. A hypothesis is a prediction of what is expected to occur by conducting the study or the relationship that is expected between the variables studied.

Specific terms in the study need to be defined. The reader of a study needs to have a clear understanding of how the terms are used and what they mean. Key terms used in the problem statement, purpose statement, and research questions, or hypotheses are the main terms that need to be defined.

The next step is a review of the literature. Past and current studies that are relevant to the study are reviewed and summarized. The reason for conducting a literature is to determine what research has already been conducted, what gaps in the research exist, and what contradictions may exist in the literature.

The literature can also provide guidance on how other researchers have approached research for this type of study.

Next we need to define who we are studying. The subjects used in the study are referred to as the sample or populations for the study.

The next step is to determine what measurements we will use in collecting data for the study. We need to be sure that the measurements that we need will be available for the study. Also we want to make sure that we can depend on the measurements to give us the data we need.

Procedures then need to be developed for conducting the study and collecting the data. Procedures are step-by-step directions that outline what will occur from the beginning to the end of the project.

Once the data are collected, the data analysis can begin. The data analysis uses statistical or qualitative procedures to analyze and explain the data. The analysis phase should provide the answers to our research questions.

Once the data analysis is completed, we then make conclusions about what we have discovered. Then we can think about the implications of what we have learned and what we will do with the information we have discovered.

These procedures seem somewhat daunting at first glance. However, if we break them down into step by step procedures, we can get from the beginning to the end of the project. The next chapters will deal with each one of the steps in more detail, with the goal being that you are equipped to carry out a research project.

Generally research is thought of as a formal process. When the goal of the research is to publish in a research journal, these steps need to be followed in detail and explained explicitly. However, the educational leader and other practitioners often conduct more informal research in order to gather information to make decisions. In these projects, the steps should be followed but may not be as explicitly stated or stated in detail as in a formal study. These procedures provide a roadmap for conducting a successful research project.

CHAPTER 3

Beginning the Research Project
Topic, Problem Statement, Purpose Statement, and Research Questions

The first step in beginning a research project is to clarify the topic. After the topic is identified, a problem statement, a purpose statement and research questions are developed. This chapter will explore the process of conducting the first steps in a research project. These steps are perhaps the most important steps in conducting research. If these are done well, the rest of the project can usually move along by building on the foundations of a good beginning. If these first steps are not done well, a well-intentioned project usually runs into trouble because of a failure to create a firm foundation for conducting the project.

1 Developing the Topic

Again the first step in a research project is to identify and focus the topic. A research topic defines the focus and scope of the study. It should also be important, relevant, and of interest to the researcher. Although these requirements may sound trite, if all three are not met, the project will have trouble from the beginning. If it is not important and relevant, there will be no use for the results at the end of the research. If it is not of interest to the researcher, the work will be drudgery for the researcher and the chances of success will be diminished. The topic should also be manageable given current skills, resources, and time available. An important task is to be sure the project is limited enough in scope that it can be successfully completed. A study that will need data to complete that will not be available for six months, but is due in one month will have no chance of success. Or if a project contemplates interviews that would have extensive costs in time and money may make the project infeasible to complete successfully. Young or inexperienced researchers often make the mistake of trying to take on more in a project than what can reasonable be accomplished. The more that the limitations are considered in the initial planning of a project, the greater the chances that the project can be successfully completed.

The topic also needs to be ethical to research. Some topics may be important and relevant, but if it can't be carried out in an ethical manner. The topic should not be pursued. Most school districts have policies in place governing research. All universities that receive federal funds and conduct research, must have Institutional Review Boards in place. It is important for the protection of human subjects as well as for the researcher to be sure that these procedures are followed.

To summarize the topic should meet the following criteria for identifying a topic:

- The topic is interesting to you.
- The topic is researchable.
- The topic has theoretical or practical importance.
- The topic should be ethical to research.

2 The Problem Statement

Once the topic is developed, the researcher needs to address the question of what is the problem that the research will investigate. This is known as the problem statement. We want to be sure before we start that the problem we have is important enough to investigate based on the criteria above. The problem statement is a statement of why the topic is an important problem to study. There is some unmet need for information that exists or a new area that needs to be researched. The problem statement is accompanied by background of the study and justification for the study.

3 The Purpose Statement

The next step is developing a purpose statement. The purpose statement is a clear, concise statement of what the study will accomplish, usually in one sentence. Spending the time on developing and refining a clear purpose statement will help guide the researcher through the details of completing the project, without getting lost in the details.

The criteria for a good purpose statement are as follows:

- Identifies the variables of interest
- Describes the specific relationship between the variables
- Identifies the nature of the participants (sample).

Examples of purpose statements include the following:

- The purpose of the study is to investigate the impact of a new mathematics curriculum on student achievement in grades 6–8.

- The topic investigated in this study was parents' beliefs about homework for primary grade children.

4   Research Questions

After the purpose statement has been written a very important step in the research process starts. That is to identify research questions. This is the first step listed in the scientific method, and is related to the research hypothesis. The research questions should flow out of the problem statement and purpose statement. First of all the questions need to be researchable. This means that the questions can be answered by collecting and analyzing data. Questions that address values and not data are not research questions as they cannot be answered by collecting data. Questions should also be clear and unambiguous. Anyone reading the questions should have the same idea of what they mean. It is important to use specific wording and not general words and phrases in developing the questions. The questions should also have theoretical or practical significance. This should have been addressed in developing the topic, but this is a good time to check and be sure. The questions can be answered ethically. Finally the questions can be adequately researched given the expertise, resources, and time constraints of the researcher.

Here are some examples of researchable questions and questions that are not researchable:

Not Researchable
- Should I enroll my child in a charter school?
- Are PLCs good for education?
- What changes should be made in the Teacher Induction Program

Researchable
- What is the evidence of student achievement on the standardized state test between charter schools and regular public schools?
- What is the impact of the implementation of a PLC in middle school on student achievement?

5   Definition of Terms

Once the purpose statement and research questions have been developed, terms used in the statements and in the study need to be defined. The reason for defining terms is so that the reader has the same understandings of what the terms mean as the researcher does. There are two types of definitions used in a research study. They are constitutive definitions and operational definitions. The constitutive definitions in a study are the typical definitions found in dictionaries. The second type of definition, the operational definition, is a definition specific to the study. The operational definition explains how the term is used in the study, and identifies specific measures or procedures that describe how the as term is used in study, and are based on and consistent with studies that have already been conducted and published in the literature.

The procedures described in this chapter are presented in a sequential manner. This sequential presentation may imply that one step is completed before the next step is begun. In reality the development of a research project is much more iterative. It is very common for the researcher to develop a topic, the problem statement, the purpose statement, and the research questions and they return to modify the topic. This back and forth is not only acceptable, it is a good process to follow to continually refine the components of the study. Once these components have been developed and refined the researcher is in a good position to proceed with a well-defined, solid understanding of what needs to be accomplished.

CHAPTER 4

Finding and Reviewing Literature for Credible Research

This chapter will be very short and will focus on finding and reviewing literature about a research topic. The section will not be a detailed analysis on finding literature or the procedures for reporting literature. It will only give a brief overview of things to look for in the literature that may compromise the credibility of what is reported. Things to be aware of include indicators of bias, sensational wording, use of value laden words, overgeneralizing conclusions, and cherry picking conclusions or data to report.

The first thing you should look for in the writing of a research report such as a journal article is to look for any indicators of bias. Bias can be either very blatant or can be very subtle. Some advertisements that one sees in the media have indicators of bias that are very blatant. This bias is also found in advertisements by vendors for particular products such as a new instructional intervention product. The claims made are often biased and unsubstantiated. You should be aware of looking for this as you read through vendor claims as well as research articles.

Research articles, especially articles that have been refereed in professional journals, are reviewed for bias before they are published. However, subtle biases can also creep in to the way authors write the reports and in the way they introduce the materials in the article. Articles can be biased in that they may be only talk about certain aspects of the literature and ignore other parts that are known. Bias could also come from very subtle wording that leads the reader towards a certain conclusion, which is not based on the literature or on the conclusions from the analysis of data.

The second issue to watch out for is what is called sensational writing. Sensational writing is often used in popular media such as newspapers or in Internet posts because they grab a person's attention. This writing plays on the emotions of the reader. Newspapers use this practice often to be able to get more readers and subscriptions. However, in good research reports, the writing should be very objective, dispassionate, and objective. You can look for these indicators of sensational writing as you review an article. The article should not contain sensational words and phrases but rather be a professionally written, objective article.

Another issue to watch out for is the use of value laden words. The use of value laden words is also related to bias and means that authors sometimes will use words that are heavily value laden instead of objective, neutral words. The reader should be aware of the use of value laden words because they can leave the reader with an impression that is not justified by the research.

Another indication of bias is what is called cherry picking. Cherry picking data means that only facts and conclusions that support the author's point of view are selected, and other facts are left out. Sometimes authors of studies will cherry pick their conclusions or the data that they will report. This is an indication of bias. It is also an unethical practice in research. You should look for indications that the research has been cherry picked or that only conclusions that support the authors' hypotheses are being reported.

Finally in the review of the literature, the reader should look for the documentation of claims that are made in the conclusions of the research report. The claims should be related to the hypotheses or questions that are asked, and they should be supported by the analysis of the results in the research. Sometimes researchers are prone to overstating the conclusions of their research. It is very important that researchers stay within the limitations of their analysis. If a result seems to be somewhat tentative, it should be stated that way in the conclusions of the report. If the reader of research is aware of these possible sources of bias, then the reader should be aware of any over generalization or limited documentation of results.

CHAPTER 5

Populations and Samples

Two major ideas will be discussed in this chapter. They are populations and samples. A population contains all of the members of a particular group that we are interested in studying. The sample is a group that we take from the population and study it directly. Then we draw conclusions about the population. In this chapter we will look at the concept of population and sampling and how it applies to a research project.

1 Identifying the Population

The population consists of all members of a particular group that is studied. The first task concerning the subjects in a research project is to define the population of interest. There are two terms we use in talking about a population. The first term is a target population. The target population is the actual population of interest we want to study and make generalizations about. The researcher will generalize to this group of people at the conclusion of a research project. The population might be all of the fourth-grade students in the United States. Another population could be all dropouts in a particular state or perhaps our population of interest could be limited to all students in a in a suburban middle school.

Most of the time but not always, the entire target population is not actually accessible so we have to go to a second version of a population; that is called our accessible population. In the examples used above we seldom have the resources to study everybody in the fourth grade in the United States. However if our study was limited to an elementary school, it would be relatively simple to access all of the fourth graders in the elementary school. The first step in a research project is to go directly to the target population. When this is not feasible we need to determine the accessible population.

The accessible population will be the group that is actually available. This population should be identified so that it most closely resembles the target population. We could say that this is our realistic choice of a population. Sometimes it is very easy to go from the target population to the accessible population such as studying the population of elementary school. However, if we were interested in studying all of the voters in a particular county, we may have some difficulties in conducting the study.

Voter registration rolls are publicly accessible, but being able to access the voters from those roles may not be possible. For example, the researcher may want to conduct a telephone survey. This would require the telephone numbers for all of the voters. Perhaps not all of the voters have telephone numbers. This would bias the study towards those who have telephone numbers. There have been famous examples of survey research that was wrong because the researchers used telephones to contact the population, and many of the people in the population did not have telephones. This discrepancy caused a bias in the research leading to erroneous conclusions.

Today most people have telephones, and it is not as much of a problem as it used to be. However a newer problem is that many people today have cell phones and do not have the traditional landline telephone. Cell phone numbers are not as accessible as the traditional landline phone numbers are, and this can also lead to a bias in accessing registered voters. Today many young people do not have land lines and rely on cell phones. The cell phone numbers are generally not in the telephone directory and would be not as accessible to the researcher. If the researcher cannot access a significant subgroup of a population, a bias may be caused in the sample. In this case, younger people would tend to be more excluded from the population sample of registered voters, thus biasing the sample toward older voters.

2   Obtaining the Population

Once we have identified our accessible population we now want to obtain our sample. Sampling is a process of selecting a number of individuals from a population. These individuals should be representative of the larger population. We want to use the results of our study to generalize to this population. In research we want to generalize beyond our sample to a larger population because this is what readers of research reports are interested in. They generally are not particularly interested in the sample that a researcher studied but would like to apply these research findings to other similar populations.

A sample may or may not represent the parent population. There are sources of error in drawing a sample from a population. These sources of error are systematic error and sampling error. Sampling error can be controlled through good sampling procedures and statistical procedures. However, systematic error cannot be controlled through statistical procedures and can cause a bias in the sample. Unfortunately the researcher usually does not know for certain how much bias exists in the sample.

There are different types of sampling strategies that are used in research. These strategies can be broken down into two basic types of sampling, random sampling and non-random sampling. Our desire overall is to have an unbiased sample, one that is representative of the parent population. A sample should represent the population as much as possible. Random sampling is a method of selecting subjects from a population by chance. This sampling procedure controls for biases in the sampling procedure. If a sample is randomly drawn, the only source of error is sampling error, and sampling error is predictable. Any differences that result between the sample and the parent population would be simply due to chance factors or sampling error and not bias. One way to control for sampling error in the selection of a sample is to include as large of a sample as possible. As the size of the sample size is increased, the sampling error will be decreased. This is true up to a point. For large populations and samples, this relationship decreases and increasing a sample size beyond a certain point becomes a matter of diminishing returns. This phenomenon will be addressed later in this chapter.

3 Types of Random Samples

There are three basic types of random sampling. The first is simple random sampling. Simple random sampling is, as its name implies, is the simplest form of random sampling. The researcher organizes the population in some method and then randomly selects members from that population.

3.1 *Simple Random Sampling*

The traditional method of doing random sampling was to use a table of random numbers. A table of random numbers can be found in the back of most statistics books and can be used to draw a simple random sample. A table of random numbers, as the name implies is a table, in which numbers are arranged on the page in a random order. In order to do a random sample using the table of random numbers, all of the members of the population should be listed and numbered. Then the researcher will randomly select the place to start in the table. The width of digits is selected that would allow for all members of the population to be considered. For example, if the population had 500 members, then three digits in the random number table must be utilized. Once the starting point has been selected, the researcher simply begins at that number and selects the member of the population corresponding to that number. Then the researcher goes down to the next number and selects that member into the sample. The researcher continues this process until the desired sample is selected.

Today with the advent of statistical software that is readily accessible such as Excel or SPSS, the researcher can use technology to select the sample for them. There is a procedure in SPSS for selecting a random sample if all of the members of the population are included in the data file. Excel also has the capability of drawing a random sample under certain conditions that the user can specify. Either way is generally a much easier way of selecting a random sample, and is what is used most of the time by researchers today.

Although simple random sampling is an unbiased way of drawing a sample from a parent population, it does have several disadvantages. The first disadvantage is that, unless one has the appropriate software it is somewhat tedious to perform the sampling procedure. A second more important reason is that simple random sampling does not ensure the representation of subgroups. If we are concerned about how subgroups are represented in our sample, we may want to get a more representative sample by using a technique called stratified random sampling.

3.2   *Stratified Random Sampling*

Stratified random sampling is a sampling method that is used so that subgroups are represented in the sample in the same proportion as in the population. The subgroups are referred to as strata. For example, let's say that a sample is drawn and represents gender, racial, and ethnic groups proportionally to the population. This would be very important, if we are interested in how males may be different from females and how one ethnic group may differ from another. The advantage of stratified random sampling is that it increases the confidence that subgroups are proportionally represented. A disadvantage of stratified random sampling is that it is more difficult to do. Not only does the researcher have to conduct the sampling as in the simple random sample above but the researcher also has to repeat this process for every subgroup in the population. Sometimes certain subgroups may not be as accessible as others, introducing a potential bias in the sampling. The advantage of stratified random sampling is that the representation of all subgroups can be ensured.

3.3   *Cluster Random Sampling*

Cluster random sampling is a third way in which a sample may be obtained from a population. Cluster samples are often used when it is difficult to access the individuals in the parent population. However, it may be easier to access groupings of the population. For example if the researcher is interested in studying church members in a community, it may be difficult to access each individual church member. However it would be relatively easy for the researcher to identify a list of churches in the community. Then the researcher could select a sample of churches and contact the selected churches. Through the selected churches, the researcher can access the members. Using a cluster sampling procedure in this scenario, the researcher would randomly select churches from the community and then contact the churches to help in accessing the individual churchgoers. This may be a much more effective way of obtaining a sample than trying to directly access the individuals.

Another way in which cluster sampling may be used would be in a high school. Let's say that the researcher is interested in conducting a study of all ninth grade students in a high school. Trying to access all ninth grade students individually could present difficult logistical problems for the researcher as well as a significant disruption of the school functions during the school day. However, it might be feasible to randomly select classes which would contain all students such as an English class. Virtually all students in the ninth grade would be taking an English class. The researcher then could select English classes at random ensuring that he or she has randomly selected the classes and that they represent the ninth-grade population. Then the researcher would conduct the study in the classes selected such as administering a survey. This procedure is often done in situations such as those just described.

Cluster random sampling works best and is most efficient when there are a large number of clusters available. The cluster becomes a sampling unit. Sometimes it is more efficient and easier to implement. The disadvantage of cluster sampling is that there is a greater chance of selecting a sample that is not representative of the population because of the fewer clusters included. Nevertheless cluster sampling is an acceptable sampling procedure.

3.4 *Systematic Random Sampling*

The final type random sample is called is called a systematic random sample. A systematic random sample was used frequently in the past but is now viewed as the weakest of random sampling procedures. In a systematic random sample, a sample is obtained by selecting every nth name in a population. For example, if the population has 100 members, and the researcher would like to select a sample of 20, then the researcher with select every 5th person from the population. Systematic sampling will usually work adequately as long as there is no pattern in how the population is organized. For example if a researcher wanted to study customer perceptions of a grocery and needed to sample days of the week to collect data, systematic sampling might lead to the research being conducted on the same day of the week every week. This procedure would obviously lead to very biased results. Overall systematic random sampling is considered a weak sampling method and is not used as much today as it was in the past.

4   Non-Random Sampling

There are other sampling strategies available that are not random sampling strategies. These strategies are called systematic sampling techniques. Sometimes systematic random sampling is not even included in random sampling strategies and is included in systematic sampling strategies. There are several types of systematic sampling, but only two will be included, convenience sampling and purposive sampling.

4.1   *Convenience Sampling*

A convenience sample is not a well-regarded sampling strategy, but is often used in research. Often it is difficult to get an adequate random sampling of subjects. In this case a convenience sample may be used. This is simply a group of individuals that are conveniently available to be studied including volunteers. An example of a convenience sample may be a study that a professor is interested in conducting. The professor then selects one of his classes and uses the class members as the sample for study. Another example may be a researcher would like to interview teachers in a school for the purpose of gathering information about a study. He then decides to interview teachers who are available in the teachers' lounge during the morning. The obvious disadvantage of this strategy is that it only includes teacher in the lounge in the morning. Teachers who come to the lounge in the afternoon and those who do not visit the lounge are excluded from the sample. This method of selection probably does not represent the population and should be avoided if possible. It is easy to see how the teachers in the teachers' lounge in the morning may not represent that school, and it is very obvious the students and one professor's class would not represent all students of the university and certainly not all young adults.

4.2   *Purposive Sampling*

Another type of non-random sampling that is more highly regarded in research is known as purposive sampling. A purposive sample is selected because individuals in a population being studied have special qualifications. These may be teacher leaders in the school, early adopters of a program, or other groups that have special qualifications. Personal judgment is used in the selection process for purposive sampling. It is the responsibility of the researcher to use good judgment in selecting the members of a purposive sample to ensure that the members selected are representative of the characteristics the researcher is studying. The main disadvantage of purposive sampling is that judgment is used in selecting the sample, which can cause biases in the sample. It is the responsibility of the researcher to document the procedures used to select the purposive sample.

5   Sample Size

What is an adequate sample size? This is a question that is often asked about sampling. It is a question that the researcher must answer in selecting a sample. The first requirement is to be sure that the sample is as unbiased as possible. The size of the sample will not overcome bias if there is bias in the selection procedures of the sample. In this case a larger sample will simply yield a larger biased sample, not accurately representing the population. Assuming that the sample is unbiased in its selection, it is better to have a larger sample than a smaller sample up to a point.

There are generally three factors that determine the sample size that is needed. The first factor is the size of the population. The second is the margin of error that the researcher is willing to tolerate, and the third factor is the statistical confidence level that the researcher would like to have in the accuracy of the sample. Calculating sample sizes is a very complex statistical technique and is beyond the scope of this text. However keeping in mind the three factors above, here are some examples of the sample that would be needed to adequately represent a population. We will assume that we want to have a margin of error of plus or minus 3 and a 95% level of confidence that the sample is accurate within that margin of error. For very large populations an adequate sample size can be drawn with a relatively small percentage of the population. For example, for an infinite size population, a sample size of 1067 would meet the criteria of a margin of error of plus or minus 3 and a 95% level of confidence. However, for a population of 10,000, 964 members would have to be selected. If the population is 1,000, 516 members would need to be selected or over half of the population. As a population gets smaller, the percentage of members of the population that would need to be selected to meet our criteria increases dramatically. For a population of 100, 92 members would have to be selected to have a sample that represents the criteria that we have set for our sample. In this case it would be pointless to select a sample of 92 from a population of 100. The researcher may as well select all members and study the population and not worry about sampling error.

To summarize this chapter we may ask the question why are good sampling procedures necessary. The main reason is that a researcher would like to be able to generalize from a sample. If the researcher can generalize from a sample to a larger population, the research has what is referred to as external validity.

Research has limited value if it cannot be generalized beyond the sample studied. If the researcher wishes to generalize beyond the study, the sample should be representative of the larger population. This representativeness of the larger population is critical for the external validity of a research project.

CHAPTER 6

Measurement of Variables

After the researcher has identified the research questions and sample, the next step is to collect data. Data refer to individual pieces of data that are obtained in some manner from subjects. After collecting the data, the researcher will need to turn the data into information. An instrument refers to the device that is used to collect the data. There are a lot of theoretical and logistical considerations that the researcher needs to take into consideration with an instrument. First, the data must be collected accurately and consistently or the data will be useless. Another consideration is how easy is it to collect the information with the instrument being used.

When deciding on using an instrument, several questions about how usable the instrument is should be addressed. One consideration is how long it will take to administer the instrument. If it will take a very long time, the length of time may be just too disruptive for the research to be conducted. Once the data have been collected, the data must be analyzed in some systematic way. Thinking up front through these issues can save a lot of time, energy, and frustration on the part of the researcher as the project progresses.

Another factor to consider is whether to use an instrument that has already been constructed or whether the researcher should develop a new instrument. Both have their advantages and disadvantages. An existing instrument may already has established validity and reliability. There may also be user experience with the instrument. In this case the researcher has an idea of what to expect when administering the instrument. However there is a major disadvantage to an existing instrument. It may not match your topic or research questions exactly. In this case you may need to modify the instrument, revise your research questions or perhaps abandon this instrument altogether. The final problem with an existing instrument is that it may be copyrighted and require permission to use the instrument. Obtaining permission may or may not be a significant problem.

If a satisfactory instrument cannot be found, it may be necessary to create an instrument. The advantage of a newly created instrument is that it can be specifically tailored to the research topic. The disadvantage is that it has to be developed from the beginning. No prior record of use exists for the instrument so all procedures and instructions have to also be developed. Also since the instrument has just been created, the researcher has the responsibility of establishing the reliability and validity of the instrument.

Another option is to use a modified instrument. A modified instrument is a combination of a created instrument and an existing instrument. Permission may also be required to modify an existing, copyrighted instrument. Another factor to consider how major the changes to the instrument are. If the changes are trivial, the instrument can be used as is with the changes. However if substantive changes are made to the content of the instrument, the researcher will need to re-establish the reliability and validity of the instrument.

Instruments can be classified into two categories. In one category, the researcher completes the instrument and in the other category the subject of the study, such as a student, completes the instrument. There are several types of instruments that are completed by the researcher. These include rating scales, checklists, observation forms, interview schedules, tally sheets, and anecdotal records. These instruments vary greatly in their purpose and in how they are used. A second type of instrument is completed by the subjects in the research study. These include surveys, attitude scales, achievement tests, aptitude tests, performance assessments, self-checklists, personality measures, and socio-metric devices.

There is another potentially very valuable source of data that the researcher should consider. This source is referred to as unobtrusive measures. Many instruments require the cooperation of the respondent. These instruments include tests, surveys, and other instruments that the subject must complete. In order to collect the data, there must be an intrusion into the research situation. Other instruments collected by the researcher also take time and may change the research setting. This intrusion can cause problems and at least change the situation. This is known as a reactive effect, and it can negatively influence the validity of the research.

Unobtrusive measures are data that are collected in a way that does not intrude on the setting for the research. These data can include already existing data such as records of test scores, grade reports, and artifacts. Artifacts are records that are results of record-keeping or activities related to the project. An advantage of unobtrusive measures is that they do not require an additional data collection procedure, and the records already exist. A second advantage is that the researcher does not have to intrude on the situation and risk influencing the results. The final advantage of unobtrusive measures is that they require no additional time or disruption of the research setting such as the classroom, and we all know that classroom time is very valuable.

Once the data are collected, the data usually have to be scored in some way. The raw score is the initial score obtained by scoring or grading the instrument. The raw score may have meaning for that particular situation, but it is difficult to interpret the meaning of the raw score outside of that particular situation or classroom. Thus, the raw score has little meaning outside of the school's classroom where the assessment was administered. To be meaningful outside of the original setting, raw scores must be standardized in some way. This standardization allows for scores to be compared to other subjects or to a standard, and are referred to as derived scores. Examples of derived scores include scale scores, percentile ranks, and proficiency levels.

Derived scores are generally reported in two different ways, norm-referenced scores and criterion referenced scores. Both types of scores give meaning to individual scores by comparing scores in some way. Norm-referenced instruments are instruments that compare scores to a norm group, such as the national average for fourth-graders. Criterion-referenced scores are scores that compare an individual score to a particular standard or criterion, such as a passing score for a performance level.

Very important concepts in the measurement of variables are the concepts of validity and reliability. Validity is an indication of whether the instrument measures what it is intended to measure. Another question that validity seeks to answer is, "Are inferences made from the instrument justified." Validity is a very important concept to consider when preparing or selecting an instrument. There are several types of validity, and the type of validity that is most important for an instrument is depends on the intended use of the instrument.

There are three major types of validity. The first type of validity is content validity. Content validity requires an analysis of the content of an instrument and a comparison of the content to the standards or learning outcomes that the instrument is measuring. A second form of validity is criterion validity, and it analyzes the relationship between the scores obtained from the instrument and some other measure. Criterion validity can be broken down into two different types of validity, predictive validity and concurrent validity. The only difference between the two is the time interval between when the instrument is administered and the criterion data are collected. The third major type of validity is referred to as construct validity. Construct validity relates to the way a concept is operationally defined for the research. Many psychological constructs that are used today such as attitude, self-concept, and anxiety are measured using construct validity procedures.

Content validity is a common form of validity used in education and is the primary type of validity used for achievement tests. Content validity is a measure of how well the test aligns with the content being measured. If an instrument has content validity, all of the items on the instrument should match one of the learning outcomes being measured. The second way of looking at content validity is comparing how much of the content being measured is covered by the test.

Some tests only measure parts of the content standards because of carelessness or some content standards are hard to measure with traditional paper and pencil tests. The test should also reflect a proportional emphasis of the content. If one particular performance standard is very heavily weighted in the content standards, it should also be heavily weighted in the test. Another aspect of content validity, is whether the taxonomy of the items are aligned with the taxonomy of the content. If content standards require application of knowledge and thinking skills, the test should also have items that require the application of these same skills. One flaw that many tests have is that they only measure lower levels of knowledge. This flaw does not occur with all tests, but it is common because it is more difficult to construct items that require higher level thinking skills. If the content standards require higher level thinking skills, the test should also require these skills to be demonstrated in order for the test to have content validity.

Criterion related validity compares assessment results with some external criterion. The external criterion should be related to the construct being measured. There are two types of criterion validity, concurrent validity and predictive validity. In each case the criterion should be closely related to what the instrument is measuring, but does not have to be the same type of measure. For example, criterion validity could be established by comparing the results of a test score to grades.

Concurrent validity compares the scores on an instrument to another measure collected at approximately the same time as when the instrument was administered. For example, an individually administered intelligence test might be compared to a group-administered test. If the group-administered test is strongly related to the individually administered test, then the user may conclude that the group administered test has validity. Under certain conditions the group administered test will yield valid results similar to the individually administered test. If the validity of the group administered test is established for a specific situation, the administration of the group administered test could require less time and expense to administer and still produce valid results.

Predictive validity compares scores on an instrument to some other measure collected at some future time. A classic example of the use of predictive validity is looking at the relationship between SAT results and college success. If there is a relationship between the SAT scores and some future indicator of college success such as freshman grade point averages, then the researcher could conclude that the SAT has predictive validity. Although this relationship sounds simple, it is a very controversial topic, and many studies have been conducted looking at this relationship.

Construct validity is another way to document the validity of an instrument. Construct validity is frequently used in the study of psychological constructs such as self-concept, motivation, and anxiety. In these measures there is no set of content standards as with achievement tests, so content validity is not very applicable. There are several ways to assess construct validity. One way to measure construct validity is to form a panel of experts that examines the instrument in relation to the underlying construct being measured. The experts assess the instrument to determine if the instrument accurately represents the construct. If they conclude that the instrument does measure the construct, it can be concluded that there is evidence of construct validity.

Another way to establish construct validity is to design a research study, develop a hypothesis based on the construct, and conduct a study to test the hypothesis. An example of a research study based on construct validity could be a study to examining the relationship between anxiety and depression. The researcher may hypothesize that subjects with high levels of anxiety also have high levels of depression. This hypothesis can be tested on a sample of subjects and a comparison is made by examining the results of the measures of anxiety and depression. If there is a relationship between the two measures as hypothesized, the researcher can conclude that there is evidence of construct validity for the measure of anxiety. A third approach to construct validity includes very advanced statistical procedures such as factor analysis. Factor analysis is well beyond the scope of this text, but is often cited in the literature as a way to measure construct validity. The procedure of factor analysis explores the underlying factors of an instrument and compares them to the constructs measured by the instrument. If the statistical factors align with the constructs of the instrument, the researcher can conclude that the instrument has construct validity.

Reliability is another major indicator of the quality of an instrument. While validity indicates how well the instrument measures what it intends to measure, reliability refers to the consistency of scores provided by the instrument. In theory, if we administered the same instrument to a subject many times without any interventions, the results should be the same or close to the same. If there is a large variation in scores, it would indicate a lack of reliability.

All measures have some degree error. The idea is to minimize the amount of error in the scores. This introduces the concept of the true score. We can conceptualize a score that we observe as containing two components, a true score and an error term. This concept is illustrated as follows:

$$O = T + e \qquad (1)$$

O represents the score that we observe, T represents the true score and e represents the error term. The only score we can actually see is the observed score. We cannot directly observe the true score or the error but must estimate them in some way. The idea of a reliable instrument is that we want to minimize the error term and maximize the true score term. If we had a perfectly reliable instrument the error term would be zero. In reality, this will never exist, but we would like to have the error term as close to zero as possible.

Similar to the validity, there are several ways of measuring reliability, and the preferred method is based on the intended use of the instrument. The major types of reliability include test-retest reliability, equivalent-forms reliability, and internal consistency.

The test-retest method requires the administration of the same instrument twice to a group after a certain time interval is elapsed. A reliability coefficient, similar to a correlation coefficient, is calculated to indicate the relationship between the two sets of scores. If the correlation is positive and high, there is good evidence that the instrument has test-retest reliability. The time between the first and second administration of the instrument depends on the situation and how the instrument is used. It is important that there is no intervention that occurs between the administrations of the instrument that could affect the scores. This method of assessing reliability is often confused with pretest-posttest scenarios. The major difference between the two techniques is whether an intervention occurs. If we are measuring the effectiveness of a program, we might administer a pretest, implement the intervention, and administer a posttest. For reliability purposes we do not want to have any interventions between the administrations. We only want to test the instrument.

Equivalent forms reliability requires the construction of two different but equivalent forms of an instrument that are administered to the same group during the same time period. This method is also called alternate forms or parallel forms reliability. They all mean the same thing. The reliability coefficient is calculated between two sets of scores. If the correlation is high, there is evidence that the two forms are measuring the same thing. The difficulty with this procedure is that two instruments must be constructed to achieve different equivalent forms. It is hard enough to construct one good instrument and doubly hard to construct two different forms of the same instrument. This form of reliability is seldom used except by major test publishing companies that desire to have multiple forms of their instrument available.

The third type of reliability requires only one administration of a single form of an instrument and is called the internal consistency method. Because only one form and one administration is required, this procedure is very often used in reliability analysis studies. Although there are earlier methods for the internal consistency approach, the major method used today is the Kuder-Richardson formulas. The most used formulas is known as KR_{20}.

The formula is based on the correlation of items within a test. Essentially a correlation is computed between each item and every other item. This forms a correlation matrix and is used to analyze and compute the KR 20 reliability coefficient. This procedure is the most often used procedure for establishing the reliability of measures today. Although the statistical calculations are beyond the scope of this text, the KR20 coefficient is often reported in the literature and in instrument documentation. KR21 is a simplified version of the KR20 formula, but is not used as much today because of the availability of high speed computers and statistical software.

The major limitation to the KR 20 formula is that it only applies to items that are scored in a right-wrong manner. If items are on a scale that has more than two options, KR 20 will not work. The alpha coefficient sometimes referred to as Cronbach's Alpha is an expanded form of the KR 20 and is used to calculate reliability of instruments that have items scored on a scale containing more than two choices. An example of such a scale would be a scale that has responses on a scale from 1 to 5 from strongly agree to strongly disagree known as a Likert scale.

An application related to reliability is called the standard error of measurement. Measurement error always exists especially in educational and social science research. The reason is that these fields study abstract concepts that cannot be physically observed are measured. This will always lead to some amount of error. The standard error of measurement is based on the reliability of an instrument. There is an inverse relationship between the reliability of an instrument and its standard error of measurement. If an instrument has high reliability, then the standard error of measurement will be smaller. The standard error indicates a theoretical range of scores that you would expect to find for a subject if the instrument was administered again under the same conditions. It is sometimes expressed as percent likelihood that the true score falls within the range of scores above and below the observed score. Many norm-referenced score reports include percentile scores using percentile bands that are based on the standard error of measurement without going into the technicalities of the calculations behind the range shown.

Another type of reliability that is used with observation records and performance type assessments is referred to as inter-rater reliability. Some experts also view inter-rater reliability is a measure of validity. A greater reliability is a reflection of the scoring agreement that multiple independent scorers achieve. If independent scorers come to the same score on an instrument, interrater reliability is established. Instruments that use direct observations or instruments that require a reader to make a judgement of the quality of a document such as a writing sample, are highly vulnerable to observer differences. Also performance test results that do not have obvious right wrong answers need to be scored using the judgement of raters. Interrater reliability is the best way to establish reliability of these instruments. If the raters agree that one response is the correct or best response, it can be concluded that that instrument has interrater reliability. This interrater reliability provides evidence that other raters trained in the instrument would make the same decisions. Once the interrater reliability is established for the instrument, training is almost always required to achieve the same level of agreement among raters as was established in the reliability study.

In this chapter concepts of instrumentation and measurement were discussed. As stated earlier, it is critical that the instrument used to collect data accurately measures the concepts being studied. If it does, accurate data can be collected for the research project. Then the data can be analyzed to effectively address the research questions in the study.

CHAPTER 7

Internal and External Validity and Threats to Validity

Internal and external validity are very important concepts in the conduct of research. This chapter will focus on concepts of internal and external validity and threats to both in a research design. When we design a research project, we want to design it in a way that ensures the highest possible internal validity. There are several threats to the internal validity of a research design, and they will be discussed in this chapter.

First of all, what is internal validity? Internal validity is the extent to which observed differences in the dependent variable are directly related to the independent variable. If a relationship is observed that is not related to extraneous variables such as differences in subjects, location, or other related factors, the research probably has strong internal validity. Internal validity has a different meaning than external validity, which was discussed earlier in Chapter 5. External validity refers to how generalizable the results of the study are beyond the sample that is actually studied. There are many threats to internal validity. Stated another way, there are many things that can go wrong in a study and lead to erroneous conclusions. These threats must be addressed in a quality study as much as possible.

1   Threats to Internal Validity

The first threat to internal validity are subject characteristics. The subject characteristics threat occurs when the selection of subjects results in differences between groups that are related to the different variables being studied. This difference can cause a selection bias. The selection bias means that something in the makeup of the subjects favors one group or another group. For example, we may be comparing a new intervention using two classes in the fourth grade in an elementary school. One of the classes may have a higher level of overall ability than the other class. If this is the case, the group that has a higher level of ability is greatly favored in the study and the study is biased against the other group.

The second threat to internal validity is mortality. Mortality refers to the loss of subjects. This loss of subjects can limit the generalizability of the research and can also introduce bias. Were the subjects lost similar or different than those who remained in the study or in the control group? We may also ask the question, "Does the treatment cause the attrition to occur?" If a treatment such as in intervention program for after school tutoring shows a positive effect for most of the students who participated, but a large percentage of the students quit in the middle of the program, what effect does this attrition have on the conclusions of the study? This attrition can detract from the conclusions about the effectiveness of the program. Any study which goes on over a longer period of time or relies on volunteers is particularly subject to the threat of mortality. In order to minimize the threat to mortality the researchers should collect information about the members of the group, their attendance, and how many actually complete the program. This will aid in explaining any attrition that occurs during the program.

Another type of threat to validity is called location. The location threat means that something about the setting or settings of the study has an effect on the outcome, either positive or negative. There are many factors that could result in a location threat, and in a research study, these factors may influence the results. These differences in location could include differences in technology between two groups, differences in teacher or staff morale, and many other factors. In order to minimize these threats of location, the researchers should try to implement the program in a way that ensures the least possible differences in the locations used in the study.

The next type of a threat to internal validity is called instrumentation. This threat refers to how instruments are used in the study, which may cause a threat to the internal validity of that study. There several ways in which an instrumentation effect may occur. One way is through what is referred to as instrument decay. The procedure for administering the instrument changes over a period of time. For example, if a person is collecting data by making observations, they may start looking for different things over a period of time. This change can cause the results of the observations to change significantly. Another way in which an instrument may decay is through the fatigue of the person administering the instrument. As the research is conducted, the data collector may get tired and then miss certain behaviors that are important for the study.

A third type of threat to the instrumentation of a study is the attitude of the subjects toward the instrument. This can be caused by something such as test fatigue of students taking the instrument. The students may feel that they are being tested too often. This feeling could cause them to get tired of having to take another test and not do their best. This change in attitude could cause the results of the study to be biased.

The fourth type of threat of instrumentation comes with the characteristics of the data collector. The appearance or actions of the person collecting the data can have an effect on the results. It is well-known that when principals or other adults enter a classroom, that their appearance can have an effect on the behaviors and the characteristics of the teacher and the students. Another example may be a policemen, who is conducting interviews with community members about the community's perceptions of law enforcement. The appearance of a uniformed officer collecting the data may cause respondents to be less than candid. Thus, the appearance of the data collector can have an effect on the results.

Another type of an instrumentation threat is data collector bias. This bias means that there is a difference in the procedures or attitudes of the data collector that affects the data collection. If a data collector has strong opinions about a particular intervention, the data collector may be biased in the way that he or she records data. It is also well-known that when teacher behaviors are observed by different administrator observers, the results of the observation can be quite different. All of these instrumentation threats can threaten the validity of a research study and need to be controlled with good data collection procedures.

The next type of internal validity threat is called testing. The testing threat generally happens when there is a pretest and a posttest administered as a part of the research study. The pretest can cause a practice effect between the pretest and the posttest. Sometimes this is a significant potential problem, and other times it may not be. If the study is conducted collecting data that can be influenced easily by the knowledge or attitude of the subjects, this threat could be serious. For example, if a researcher is conducting a study of anxiety, the administration of a pretest measuring anxiety may have an influence on how the subjects in the study react to the treatment as well as how they respond only posttest.

In other situations, the testing threat may not be a major problem. If the outcomes that are being studied in a project have to do with student achievement, having a pretest is often considered a good practice and could often be a part of the normal implementation of the program. In this case any change that occurs could be a result of the implementation of a program that uses a pretest and not a threat to the validity of the study.

The next type of threat to validity is history. A history threat occurs when there is an event that occurs during the course of the study that affects the outcome. This may be something that cannot be foreseen but can, in any case, have an influence on the results of the project. An example may be that in a study comparing two classroom interventions that is highly supported by the principal, the principal leaves in the middle of the study. This event may have a big influence on the conduct of the study and of the results that occur. Sometimes this historical event only happens in one group. This is referred to as local history. Local history means that something happened to one of the groups that are being studied but not in the other group. An example of this threat occurring could be a teacher who is implementing the program decides to resign. This could obviously have a major effect on the conduct and outcome of the study in that class.

Another threat to the validity of a study is called maturation. The maturation threat is associated with the passing of time rather than the intervention that is being studied. For example, if a study takes place in an elementary school over the period of a year, we would expect that students would grow, develop, and mature. Conducting a study looking at growth over a period of time, especially with younger children, would not be very valid without having a control group to compare their growth to the experimental group. Without having a good control group, subjects could simply be maturing or developing during the course of the study independent of the intervention that is being studied.

The next type of threat to validity is the attitude of the subjects in the study. When this threat occurs, the attitude that subjects in the study exhibit can have an effect on the outcome of the study. Industrial psychologists in the early 20th century were very interested in studying the efficiency of workers and how to improve their efficiency. Many of these studies were conducted in the town of Hawthorne, New Jersey. In one series of studies the researchers improved the lighting conditions for a group of workers by making the lights brighter. As a result of change in the lighting, the productivity of this group of workers increased. However when the study was redone and the lighting was made less bright, the productivity of the workers also increased. The workers being studied knew that they were part of an experiment, and thought that they were special, which caused their productivity to go up regardless of the lighting conditions. Other studies found similar conclusions, and this phenomenon became known as the Hawthorne effect.

It is certainly possible that subjects may perform better based upon a feeling that they are receiving special attention. In education if we identify students for a special program, they are made to feel special. They may have a more positive attitude and perform better in whatever it is that they are being asked to do. The opposite may also occur. When subjects are receiving a "bad" treatment, or they feel stigmatized, the subjects may have a bad attitude and not perform as well as they could. It is important that the researcher be aware of the attitude of those participating in the study and ensures that any attitudes that exist do not bias the results of the study in an unintended way.

Another type of threat to internal validity is called statistical regression or sometimes referred to as regression to the mean. A regression threat may exist when changes are studied in a group that has extreme high or low performance. The regression effect only occurs if the selection of the groups is based on extreme scores. An example of this phenomenon would be when students are selected into an intervention group based on low scores on the end of year test. The phenomenon of regression to the mean occurs if subjects for a study are selected based on extremely low scores such as the end of year test. If these subjects were then administered the same test again, the results would almost always increase.

This phenomenon occurs because of a lack of perfect reliability in the assessment. The factors that led a student to get a very low score were partially attributable to the unreliability of the test. Since only extreme scores were selected, the unreliability tended to be more on the negative side. Upon a second administration, the unreliability errors would be randomly distributed and not in any particular direction. If there is no control group of subjects that are selected in the same way but do not receive the intervention treatment, there is a serious threat that the changes that occur in these groups will be at least partially because of the regression to the mean effect and not because of the intervention. This problem can occur with remedial programs, but it can also occur in programs where students are selected who have very high scores. This regression to the mean effect occurs for extreme scores that are selected, either high or low scores.

The next type of threat to internal validity is implementation. An implementation threat can occur when the experimental group or the control group are treated in unintended ways giving them an advantage or disadvantage. This effect can occur in two ways. The first is when a study comparing two groups, and different individuals are assigned to implement two different methods. These individuals then differ in ways related to the outcome. For example, the experimental and control groups have individuals implementing the study who have different levels of experience or expertise. If the individuals implementing the program are inexperienced or less skilled teachers, they could bias the outcomes against the program that they are implementing. The second way in which an implementation bias may occur is when some individuals have a personal bias in favor one method over the other. For example, a teacher may be assigned to implement a particular teaching method. If this teacher is an enthusiastic advocate for this method, and she is assigned to the experimental group, she may provide an advantage to the experimental group. By the same token if he is hostile toward this method and does not like using it, he may provide a disadvantage to the experimental group.

In this section, many ways have been discussed in which the internal validity of a research project can be threatened. The researcher should try to minimize the threats to internal validity through the design of the research study and the procedures used to implement the study. There are four strategies that can be used to reduce the threats to internal validity. The first strategy is to randomize groups if at all possible or at least ensure that they are as equivalent as possible. The second way to minimize the threat to internal validity is to standardize the conditions of the study. As much as possible all groups should be under the same conditions. The researcher should think through what could possibly go wrong and, to the extent possible, design procedures to prevent these events from occurring. The third method is to obtain detailed information on the subjects in the study. This detailed information prior to the beginning of the study can identify potential threats to validity because of the subjects selected for the study. The other reason to obtain detailed information on the subjects is to document how equivalent the groups are at the beginning of the study, especially if the randomization of groups does not occur. The fourth and final technique that a researcher can use is to choose the best possible design for the project.

Research designs will be discussed in the next chapter. Some research designs address virtually all of the threats to internal validity while other research designs address very few if any of the threats to validity. By understanding the threats to internal validity, the reader can distinguish between well designed studies that merit serious consideration and those whose validity is questionable.

CHAPTER 8

Research Designs and Their Limitations

Research and research designs that accompany them can generally be broken down into five different categories. These categories include experimental research designs, correlational research designs, causal-comparative research, survey research, and action research. This chapter will describe the different types of designs and critique their relative advantages and disadvantages. The best research designs will address virtually all of the threats to internal validity that were discussed in the last chapter. Unfortunately some research designs address very few of the threats to internal validity.

1   Experimental Research Designs

The first types of research are experimental research designs. Experimental research involves the manipulation of an independent variable, sometimes referred to as the treatment variable. It looks at the effect on the dependent variable or the outcome. In experimental research the researcher can examine the relationship of variables in terms of their cause and effect.

One of the requirements of experimental research is the random assignment and random selection of individuals for the treatment. Random assignment and random selection were discussed earlier in Chapter 5. Random assignment means that every individual in the experiment has an equal chance of being assigned to either the experimental group or the control group. This assignment is very important to internal validity. Random selection means that every member of the population has an equal chance of being selected to be a member of the sample, which will then be subdivided into the experimental and control group. The selection process is very important for external validity. Experimental research can control many of the threats to the validity of an experiment. It is the responsibility of the researcher to control for threats to internal and external validity.

1.1   *True Experimental Designs*
The first type of experimental research is referred to as true experimental designs. For a research design to be a true experimental design, there must be random assignment of subjects to the treatment and control groups. Random assignment is a powerful tool for controlling threats to internal validity. Four

types of randomized experimental designs will be discussed first. They are the randomized posttest only control group design, the randomized pretest-posttest control group design, the randomized Solomon four group design, and the factorial design.

The randomized posttest only control group design means that subjects are randomly assigned to either an experimental or control group. Then the treatment is conducted for the experimental group. After the treatment is completed, a posttest is administered to the subjects. The posttest measures any differences that may exist between the two groups on the dependent variable or the outcome of the study. The researcher then analyzes the data to determine if there was a difference in the results for the experimental group compared to the control group.

The next type of design is called the pretest-posttest control group design. This design is very similar to the posttest only design except that a pretest is added to the design. The pretest is administered after subjects are randomly assigned to the groups to get an indication of the level of performance of both groups before the experiment is conducted. The pretest has an advantage of determining if there are any significant differences between the experimental and control groups before the study begins. Then the treatment is administered to the experimental group and at the end a posttest is administered to both the experimental group and the control group. Another advantage of the pretest-posttest design is that not only can the researcher determine if there is a difference between experimental and the control group, but also can determine how much of a change or how much growth there was between the pretest and the posttest. This type of design is very desirable in education because we usually want to know not only if there is as a difference between groups but also how much of a change actually occurred or how much growth occurred between the pretest and the posttest.

The only disadvantage of the pretest-posttest control group design compared to the posttest only design, is that there can be a threat to internal validity called the testing threat. As was discussed in an earlier chapter, this threat can occur when there is an interaction between the pretest and the treatment. If the intervention is dealing with an academic outcome, this threat may not be a serious issue. However, the researcher must determine if the results of the study would be just as valid if there had not been a pretest administered. If this is the case, the researcher can be confident in the internal validity of the design and also have the benefit of being able to assess the growth or change of the subjects during the treatment.

The next type of design is a combination of both of the above designs. It is referred to as the randomized Solomon four group design. In this design four groups are used. Two receive the pretest, and two groups are not pretested. Two groups receive the treatment, and two do not receive the treatment. This combination is a combination of the posttest only design and the pretest-posttest design. In a sense this is the best of all possible worlds. The results between two groups that did not have a pretest can be observed as well as the difference between two groups that did have the pretest. The researcher can see also if the pretest made a difference. Although there are significant advantages to the Solomon four group design, the main disadvantage is that it doubles the amount of resources needed to conduct the study. It is difficult enough to conduct an experimental research design using only two groups for comparison, compared to a design that requires four groups.

The fourth type of design is an addition to any one of the three above designs. It is a factorial design and can be used to study the influence of more than one variable at one time. For example, we may be interested in studying the effects of a new reading program. We also may be concerned about the effectiveness of the program between boys and girls. It is possible that a program may be effective with one group but not the other group. Thus, we would add gender as a moderator variable and develop a factorial design (refer to Table 8.1).

The factorial design would have four groups. Two of the groups would be divided into males and females. Then the males and females would be subdivided into a treatment group and a control group. This means that there would be a treatment group for males and a treatment group for girls. In this design the researcher can assess the difference between the treatment group and the control group and the difference between the two gender groups. The researcher can also look to see if there is an interaction between the treatment and gender. This interaction could occur if the treatment is effective with one group more than it is with the other group. This factorial design can be an additional factor added to any of the above research designs and allows the researcher to study the effect of not only the independent variable but also a moderator variable.

TABLE 8.1   *Reading intervention program results by gender*

	Method A	Method B	Total
Male	Results	Results	
Female	Results	Results	
Total			

The designs described above are all very strong experimental designs. However, it is very difficult to carry out these types of designs outside of a laboratory. It is very difficult to conduct random assignment in field research such as in schools. Schools use many factors to schedule students into classes. Very seldom can two classes be considered randomly assigned classes. Much research today uses research designs that are considered weak experimental designs. Weak experimental designs do not control well for threats to internal validity. Examples of these designs are called the one-shot case study, the one group pretest-posttest design, and the static group comparison design.

1.2 Weak Experimental Designs

The one-shot case study is a very simple design in which a single group is selected and exposed to a treatment. There is no random assignment and no control group. After a treatment the effects of the treatment are assessed. An example of this type of design might be a teacher who teaches a unit and administers a test at the end of the unit. After grading the test, the teacher concludes that the students learned the material well or did not learn the material well. There are many threats to this type of design. We don't know how much knowledge the students had before instruction. We also cannot tell how much of the students' knowledge was because of the instruction of the teacher and how much was because of other factors outside of the teacher's instruction.

The next type of weak experimental design is the one group pretest-posttest design. In this design a single group is selected and measured both before and after a treatment. The researcher then determines if there was a change in the dependent variable between the pretest and the posttest. This is also a very weak design although it does examine how much change occurred between the beginning and end of the treatment. However many other threats to internal validity are not addressed because there is no comparable control group involved in the study.

The next type of design in this category is the static group comparison design. In this design two groups that have not been randomly assigned receive two different treatments. One group receives the treatment, and the other group is the control group. At the end of the treatment data are collected to determine if there was a difference in the results between the two groups on the dependent variable. This design, although it does allow for a comparison between the two groups, is also subject to many threats to internal validity.

There are several problems with the internal validity of the designs that are called weak experimental designs. These threats include subject characteristics, location, data collector bias, history, maturation, implementation, and statistical regression. Basically there are very few controls for the threats to internal validity in these designs, and the results of research using these designs is very limited in the conclusions that can be made from this research.

2 Correlational Research

Another type of research is correlational research. Sometimes it is either not feasible or ethical to conduct experimental research. In this case correlational research is often used. It investigates the relationship between two variables. There is no manipulation of variables used in correlational research. The result of the research is to establish if there is a relationship between two variables, and if there is, how strong is the relationship. One major disadvantage of correlational research is that it is difficult to establish cause and effect relationships between variables as is possible with experimental research.

The purpose of correlational research is to explain relationships. One can also predict one variable based on another variable. This application of correlational research is referred to as a prediction study. The variable used to make the prediction is the predictor variable, and the variable that is predicted is the criterion variable. Scatterplots, regression lines, and correlation coefficients are used to predict a score on a criterion variable. The prediction is seldom exact; there is almost always some error in the prediction.

3 Causal-Comparative Research

A related type of correlational research is called causal-comparative research. This is a special type of correlational research. In this research an attempt is made to find the cause for differences that already exist between groups of individuals. The independent variable either cannot be manipulated or for some reason it is not. Usually this type of research is used when there are either practical or ethical limitations to conducting an experimental study. Many studies in education, public health, and sociology are causal comparative in nature. Studies of differences between already formed groups such as gender, race/ethnic group, socioeconomic status, or some other condition. One example of causal-comparative research could be a study that looks at the effects of pre-kindergarten programs. Parents decide whether or not their child will go to a pre-kindergarten program. Children are certainly not randomly assigned to a program. The researcher uses data to determine if a link exists between the pre-kindergarten experience and the outcomes expected from the program.

There are several distinctions between experimental research and Causal-comparative or correlational research. These distinctions are summarized in the table below. Causal-comparative research looks at relationships and attempts to explore phenomena. It may also identify worthy studies for experimental research. A key factor in causal-comparative research is that there is no manipulation of variables. It uses relationships among variables to attempt to explore causation.

In experimental research the independent variable is manipulated. Because of the manipulation of the variable in the controlled experimental setting, stronger evidence of causation can be established. The researcher can assign subjects to treatment groups. There is also greater flexibility in the design of an experimental research. If possible, the researcher would always prefer to conduct experimental research rather than causal-comparative research or correlational research. However this may not be possible because of ethical or practical limitations of carrying out an experimental study.

There are several threats to internal validity in causal-comparative research. The biggest threat is caused by the lack of a manipulation of variables and a lack of randomization. This lack of randomization and manipulation of variables creates several possible threats. The subject threat is a major threat. Groups may not be equivalent because they may differ on certain significant factors other than the variable studied. One way to control for an extraneous variable is to match subjects on that variable from the two groups that are studied. The researcher should try to ensure that the groups are equivalent. Location is also a threat. The two groups that are compared may be in different locations. The different locations may have situations and events that make the two groups differed from each other and not comparable. See Table 8.2 for a summary comparison of causal-comparative research with experimental research.

TABLE 8.2 *Causal-comparative research vs. experimental research*

Causal-comparative research	Experimental research
– Examine relationships	– Requires manipulation of independent variables
– Explain meaning of relationships	– Often assign subjects to treatment and control groups
– Explore possible cause and effect relationships	– Researcher can design research study
– Relationships found may be caused by other variables	– Provides stronger evidence of cause and effect relationships

4 Survey Research

Another major type of research is called survey research. The purpose of survey research is to use surveys to describe a population. Surveys can be used to describe the characteristics of a large population. In a survey the researcher can ask many questions. However a survey is limited in the depth of detail and depth of questioning that can be done. It is also limited in analyzing why an observed result exists. In this section we will look at the survey as a type of research.

There are several steps that the researcher needs to take in conducting survey research. The first step is to define the problem or to determine the purpose of conducting the survey. This process is very similar to the process described earlier about determining a purpose statement for a research study. After the problem has been defined, the next step for the researcher is to identify the target population or sample. The population and sample were described earlier in Chapter 4.

The next step is to determine how data will be collected through the survey. One method of collecting data is through a direct administration of a survey. In a direct administration the survey is administered directly to a group of people in a face-to-face or live format. The survey is distributed, respondents complete the survey, and the surveys are collected all in one location directly from the respondents. The main advantage of this data collection method is that the researcher has a "captive audience' and can control the situation. A high response rate is typical for this type of survey administration.

Another way in which surveys are administered is through the mail. In this process the population or sample to be surveyed is identified and the mail addresses for each respondent is obtained. Then the surveys are mailed individually to each respondent. Respondents complete the surveys and mail them back to the researcher, usually with a self-addressed, stamped envelope, addressed to the researcher.

Another type of survey uses the telephone to conduct surveys. In this type of survey the population or sample to be surveyed is identified along with their telephone numbers. The participants are contacted by the researcher or an assistant, and the survey is administered over the telephone.

A survey can also be conducted face-to-face through personal interviews between the researcher and the survey participant. In order to conduct this type of survey, the sample of participants must be identified and arrangements must be made for a face-to-face meeting between the researcher and the respondent. In this survey procedure the researcher directly asks the survey questions of the participant and records the answers either through a recording or on paper.

The final method of collecting surveys, and one that is very often used today, makes use of the Internet and e-mail to conduct surveys. This type of survey has become very common, and there is indeed a proliferation of Internet based surveys that we all have encountered. The reason that they are so common now is that they are so easy and inexpensive to conduct. The survey is constructed often using some type of survey software. Respondents are identified usually through email, and the survey is sent to them. The respondent completes the surveys. The surveys are then either sent back to the researcher through email or simply completed on the survey software.

After the mode of data collection has been determined, the next step in the survey process is to select the sample. Selecting a sample was described in detail in Chapter 4. This process will not be described again here but uses the procedures identified in in Chapter 4. After the sample is selected, the researcher identifies the contact information for the sample members who will participate in the survey.

After the sample has been selected, the researcher must determine what item types should be used to ask the survey questions. The item types are basically closed-ended items or open-ended items. A closed-ended item is one in which the respondent selects from a choice of items. This type of item could be a yes/no type item or it could be an item that has multiple choices for responses. An open-ended item is an item where the respondent must make a written or oral response to the item. This response could be either just a few words or it could be several sentences depending on the question asked in the survey.

The next step in developing a survey is to organize the format of the survey and actually prepare the survey instrument itself. This development includes an introduction, necessary directions, and the items themselves. The items must be developed in a way that makes the survey clear and easy to understand and follow. The survey should also make an attractive appearance and engage the reader.

After the survey has been developed it needs to be pretested with a group of people similar to the final survey sample. The purpose of the pretest is to be sure that the survey works. This means that items are clear to readers, directions are clear, and the researcher receives the information that he or she was attempting to collect. Very often it is the case that something that is clear to the writer may not be clear to the reader, or may be interpreted in a different way. A good pretest of the survey will most likely eliminate any problems of unclear or misleading items and ensure that the researcher actually obtains the data necessary for the research project.

Finally once the survey has been developed and pretested it is ready for administration. A cover letter with directions needs to be developed if it is going to be sent to users by mail or through a computerized survey program. Administrative procedures also need to be developed and either incorporated into a cover letter or develop for the use of those administering the survey in a face-to-face or telephone environment. Careful attention to the administrative details of the survey will prevent unnecessary problems of administration from occurring and maximize the chances of good survey results.

It is very important in the survey that the appearance of the survey is appealing to the respondents. The item should be carefully constructed to be sure that the items are clear and understandable for all respondents. The survey should be well designed, organized, and error free. These characteristics enhance what is known as the face validity of an instrument. Face validity simply means that the reader, upon first glance at the survey, has a positive sense of the value of the survey. This face validity will help invite people to respond and increase the likelihood of a high response rate.

There are several threats to validity in survey research. In most approaches to surveys not everyone who receives a survey responds to the survey. The lack of response in surveys can be a serious problem. If there is only a small response rate, the researcher cannot be certain if the respondents represent the sample that was surveyed.

There are several ways in which the researcher can try to increase the response rate. The first one is to carefully develop the survey using the procedures discussed above. In addition to careful preparation, the researcher may send reminders to those who have not yet responded to the survey. The researcher can appeal to the conscience of the respondent in the reminders to complete the survey. Sometimes researchers will offer rewards or incentives to encourage higher participation. This can be an effective way of getting greater participation, but often it is not feasible to implement. Whatever the limitations the researcher has, he should make every attempt to get a high response rate. Otherwise the lack of response can be a serious threat to the validity of the survey.

In general there are four main threats to the internal validity of surveys. The first one is mortality. Mortality in survey research is demonstrated through non-responses. The researcher should ask why there were non-responses. Were they because of a fear of responding or perhaps just apathy on the part of the respondents? A second threat to a survey is location. A location threat occurs when the survey is conducted in a setting that can have an effect on the results. If a survey about a teacher is conducted in the teacher's classroom while the teacher is present, this location could affect how students respond to the survey. Another threat to the internal validity of survey research is instrumentation. The entire research project rests on how good the survey is. If the instrument, in this case the survey, is not a high-quality instrument, then the data collected may not be accurate, and may not reflect the viewpoints and opinions of the respondents. A related threat is called instrument decay. If a survey is repeated on numerous occasions, the respondents may grow tired of the instrument, or researchers conducting the survey may grow tired of the procedures and cause the quality of the data collection procedures to be compromised. Any of these problems can have a very significant effect on the validity of the survey responses.

5 Action Research

The next type of research is referred to as action research. Action research is different from other types of research in that it is often conducted by professional practitioners and not always by professional researchers. Action research is conducted to solve a problem or obtain information to inform a local practice. There is little if any concern in action research about generalizability or external validity. The main goal and usually the only goal of action research is to improve practice. Action research does not require a complete mastery of research methods like other methods do. An educated practitioner using some very basic procedures can often complete a very high quality action research study.

The action researcher generally will ask the following questions in conducting an action research study.

– What question do I want to answer?
– How can I answer the question?
– What data do I need to collect to answer the question?
– How do I analyze the data?
– What do the results tell me?
– What implications do the results have for my practice?
– What actions should I take based on the results?

Once the action researcher has worked through the seven guiding questions, he may have made discoveries that can improve professional practice. The concept of action research fits in very nicely with the current emphasis on professional learning communities. These communities are designed to have professional discussions that lead to improved practice. By incorporating action research into these practices, there can be a research basis for changes in practices and improvements in procedures.

There are several advantages to action research. First, the researcher does not need to be an expert in research methodology. Second, it can help improve educational practice and decision making. It can also help to identify problems in a systematic manner that can then be addressed through actions or further research. It can also help build a professional community of research-oriented practitioners. Action research also enhances reflective practice, and enhances data driven decision making.

There are threats to validity of action research. Action research requires that the researcher is just as objective and unbiased as in any other type of research. A biased practitioner is not going to get unbiased results even from the best of research. The possibilities of threats to internal validity are also present in action research. However, because the procedures are localized and less formal in nature, the threats are not as severe as with more formal, professional research efforts. Action research is also not very generalizable. The research is conducted in a local setting for a local audience to use and is not intended to be generalized to larger audiences. Even though the external validity of action research is low, this is not a major concern because generalization to a wider population is not the goal of action research.

6 Single Subject Designs

There is another type of research design that is very different from the previous designs discussed. Most comparative research compares the results of two or more groups. It is desirable to have the largest groups feasible for the study for generalization purposes. Sometimes finding large groups of individuals with the characteristics needed for research is either infeasible or even not possible. In this case single-subject research designs may be preferable to group comparisons. Single subject designs rely on data collection from a few individuals over a period of time. These designs are often used when available populations are small such as exceptional student groups or other small populations.

Results of single subject designs are usually graphed in some way with a line graph to present the data and illustrate the effects of the treatment on the individual over time. At the beginning of the study, data are collected that measure the desired outcome or dependent variable. The data are collected for a period of time to establish a baseline before a treatment occurs. Once the baseline has been established, the treatment or the independent variable is implemented and data continue to be collected to show if there is a change in the outcome behavior. After the implementation of the treatment and after the collection of data, the data points are graphed to represent what happened after the treatment. Since the same individual is followed over a period of time before the treatment and after the implementation of the treatment, the subject serves as his or her own control group.

The simplest type of single subject design is known as the A – B design. In this design data are collected from the same subject under two conditions, the baseline and the treatment. This design is the simplest of the single subject designs and simply looks at the results before, during, and after treatment. An extension of the A – B design is the A – B – A design. In this design, the baseline is established, the treatment is implemented, and later the treatment is the withdrawn. Data continue to be collected and displayed in a graph. This design allows for comparison data before treatment, during treatment, and after the treatment has been withdrawn. This design is useful to see if the treatment needs to be maintained or if the subject can continue to maintain the desired behaviour without the treatment being continuously administered.

There are threats to the internal validity of a single subject design. A significant threat to a single subject design is data collector bias. The validity of the designs rest on the capability and integrity of the data being collected. If the data collector is biased, the data could easily be flawed and cause misleading results. Implementation is also a major issue in that the design rests upon the quality of the implementation. If the implementation is flawed, the results will probably be disappointing and may not indicate the potential of the treatment. Maturation can also be a threat. If the subjects, such as young children, are the focus of the study, they may simply mature during the process of implementation regardless of the treatment. Finally, attitude can be a threat. If the subjects have a positive attitude toward the treatment, they may show improvement regardless of the effectiveness of the treatment. On the other hand, if they have a negative attitude, the attitude could affect the treatment in a negative direction.

Single subject designs also have weak external validity. Although the researcher can be relatively confident in the results of a well-designed single subject study, the generalizability of the study is very weak because only one subject is studied. It is absolutely not appropriate to generalize from one single subject study to an entire population. Replication is even more important with single subject studies than with comparison group studies. Single subject studies must be replicated several times before generalizations can begin to be made. However after several replications the researcher can begin to make generalizations from single subject studies. The value of single subject studies that have been carefully done and replicated is that they can be conducted with small populations, which may be impossible to study using more traditional group comparison designs.

CHAPTER 9

Qualitative Research

Qualitative research is a type of research that is often considered to be an alternative to traditional forms of research. It is also sometimes used in conjunction with traditional quantitative research to supplement and enrich research studies. Qualitative research studies focus on gaining insights and understandings rather than drawing conclusions about cause and effect. Little emphasis is placed on experimental control or causation. Also there is little, if any, use of quantitative data or statistical analysis. More emphasis is placed on verbal descriptions and narratives than conclusions. The differences between qualitative and quantitative research are based both on differences in methods and in philosophical approaches to the research. This chapter will explore the characteristics of qualitative research both from the perspective of philosophical differences and methodological differences.

Qualitative research emphasizes the natural setting as a direct source from which to obtain data directly and to directly obtain insights to describe the setting or situation that is being studied. While quantitative research uses research questions and collects numerical data for analysis, qualitative research generally relies more on the written word or other visual or auditory representations of data. While quantitative research seeks to draw firm conclusions about the data observed, qualitative research generally focuses on the descriptions of situations and limits the conclusions to what has been observed and how it occurred, not on why something may have occurred. Qualitative research often does not set out with a specific purpose or research questions. The qualitative approach focuses more on immersion in a situation, collection of observations, and construction of an explanation of the observations.

There are also differences in the paradigms or world view between quantitative and qualitative research. The paradigm shapes how one's philosophy and theoretical approach to research and how one approaches an investigation. Quantitative research approaches are associated with the philosophy of logical positivism. It relies on empirical data and deductive reasoning to explain phenomena. This may sound familiar as the scientific method. The scientific method has guided the development of traditional quantitative research for over a hundred years.

Qualitative approaches to research are associated with the philosophy of post modernism and presents a reaction against traditional research principles. While the scientific method, based on positivism, attempts to discover and understand basic principles in nature, postmodernism denies the existence of underlying principles of scientific truth that explain the world. In the postmodernist philosophy, reality is constructed in the mind of the individual. Postmodernism resists the notion of universal truths and principles. Although many in education may be unfamiliar with the philosophy of postmodernism, the learning theory of constructivism is closely related postmodernism. Often curriculum and instructional strategies are based on the constructivist approach to learning. The constructivist approach contends that learners construct their own meaning of knowledge when learning something new and of the world around them in general. The learning of a concept is individual to the reality of the concept constructed by the learner. In constructivist learning theory, there are few absolute and universal concepts learned and these are general relatively unimportant of trivial learnings.

The development of the entire research project is different with qualitative research compared to the scientific method used in traditional quantitative research. In quantitative research questions or hypotheses are developed at the beginning of the study and then the researcher develops procedures to answer the questions or test the hypotheses. In qualitative research, questions or hypotheses generally evolve during the study. The researcher may not know exactly what the study will yield and specific questions may limit the scope to the project too much and cause important findings and insights to be missed. At the beginning the phenomenon to be studied is identified and preliminary general questions or objectives are developed. These general questions are deliberately designed to not be specific so as not to limit the researcher in his or her observations.

Data collection is a process of continual observation over a period of time. Data analysis of qualitative data consists mostly of verbal summaries and a synthesis of qualitative data. Interpretations and conclusions evolve as data are collected and analyzed. Generally quantitative research is conducted in a linear fashion from the development of a problem statement and purpose statement to final conclusions. Although the process may be somewhat iterative in quantitative research, it is much more so in qualitative research. Often data will indicate that the researcher should change a research question or hypothesis while the study is being conducted.

One major difference in the procedures used in qualitative research is in the selection process of individuals to study. Subjects are very rarely identified for the study through random sampling. Another type of sampling called purposive sampling is mostly used as a sampling strategy instead of random sampling.

Purposive sampling is often used in qualitative research. There are several ways in which purposive sampling can be conducted. However none of them use random sampling as a strategy. Rather the strategy used in purposive sampling is to select members of a sample based on certain characteristics that the members may have. Several methods of obtaining purposive samples have been identified and are used to obtain samples for particular purposes.

1   Types of Purposive Sampling

A typical sample consists of the most typical members of a population. This might be considered your "average Joe" for representing the population being studied. The researcher attempts to find people that are typical and representative of the population.

A second type of purposive sample is a critical characteristics sample. The critical characteristics sample consists of those who have special characteristics that are critical for the study. In the sample the researcher may look for the best examples of what is being studied, such as informal leaders, early adopters, opponents, or opinion leaders. Often in education when a new initiative is being implemented, some teachers will adapt to the change or innovation quickly while others may resist. The researcher may wish to sample the early adopters of an initiative because they will have the best knowledge and experience about how the initiative is being implemented. Others may be less informed or knowledgeable and not be able to provide as much useful information to the researcher.

Another type of purposive sample is a homogeneous sample. In a homogeneous sample, the researcher wants to find people who have a common trait or characteristic or represent a specific demographic, or perhaps have a particular talent. For example, if the researcher is specifically interested in the reactions of low performing readers to a reading program, he or she might select a sample of this subgroup for interviews.

Another type of sample is an opportunistic sample. An opportunistic sample consists of individuals who happened to have had an experience with something that is being studied. They may be witnesses to an event or were especially involved in some event that happened. They may be witnesses to some major event such as a riot.

A maximal variation sample is another type of sample sometimes used in purposive sampling. The researcher tries to obtain the sample that gets the perspective from all parts of the population. All viewpoints of members of the population, even extreme views, are desired in the sample. This type of sample would be for the purpose of getting a wide perspective on perceptions, or an attempt to get the various extreme views of the population.

The final type of purposive sampling is a snowball sample. Snowball samples are often used with populations that are hard to access. It may be impossible to get a large number of members of this population to participate at one time. However, the researcher may be able to access a few people in that population and collect data from them. These persons provide the beginning of a sample. They may be able to lead the researcher to other members of the population who may be willing to participate in the study. This type of sampling is used for populations that are difficult to obtain such as gang members, homeless people, or other groups that don't readily congregate together. As more and more individuals are identified and included in the study, the sample snowballs as the name implies.

All of these types of purposive samples can provide useful data for the researcher. They all have their advantages and uses. Sometimes this type of sampling is the only feasible way to collect data. However, these are not randomly drawn samples so they do not necessarily represent the views of the entire population. Unlike random sampling where the sampling error is predictable, one can never be certain how representative the purposive sample is of the overall population. A second difference compared to a random sample is that selection requires judgement on the part of the researcher in selecting the sample. This human factor opens up the possibility of bias in the selection of the sample. Because of these factors, caution needs to be used in generalizing findings beyond the sample selected.

2   Validity in Analyzing Data

Validity is also a very important concept in qualitative research. Validity is approached differently in qualitative research than in quantitative research. One important technique used by qualitative research is cross-checking data from various sources. If data are consistent across various sources such as various people interviewed, the researcher can have more confidence that the research conclusions will be valid. Another type of cross checking is to compare data between different types of information such as archival records, interviews, and surveys. This crosschecking of information across data sources is sometimes referred to as the triangulation of data. Triangulation of data means that data are checked and cross checked across multiple methods or subjects. Agreement or disagreement from various stakeholders is assessed. For example, teachers in different categories may have similar or differing perceptions about a particular issue. Also principals may have different perceptions about an issue than teachers. This agreement or disagreement among stakeholders and data sources is very important for the researcher and will greatly affect how the researcher develops conclusions in the study.

A second method of analyzing data is to develop categories to summarize the data while reviewing the data. The researcher often tallies frequency of responses in categories or in themes. The researcher reads through materials and constructs categories or themes in which to tally responses. As the data are analyzed, responses are tallied in the categories that were developed. Sometimes the categories are considered themes if the categories lend themselves to a more abstract interpretation. After the data have been coded into the categories, the researcher examines the frequency of responses.

By systematically analyzing and categorizing the data, the researcher can maintain an organized and systematic analysis and prevent bias from creeping into the analysis. The categories that have the most responses should be noted as well as those who have fewer responses. Just because one interviewer makes one statement very passionately does not mean it can or should be generalized to all of the stakeholders being interviewed. The researcher must use caution not to overstate the meaning of any one opinion. These frequencies of responses should weigh heavily on the final conclusions that the researcher draws from the qualitative data to ensure the validity of conclusions.

Generalization of results must be approached with more caution in qualitative research. In qualitative research no attempt is made to control extraneous variables or to maintain experimental control. Usually there is no manipulation of independent variables as there is an experimental research. The main analysis in qualitative research is a description of what has been observed. Despite the best precautions that the researcher may take, conclusions are limited by the perspective of the observer. The observations are limited to what the observer sees through his or her lens. Generalizations in qualitative research are seldom justified by the results of one study. Therefore replication of qualitative studies is even more important than in quantitative studies before valid generalizations should be made.

3 Combining Methods and Mixed-Methods Research Designs

There is a significant amount of debate in the research community about the possibilities of combining qualitative research with quantitative research. There are two main viewpoints about the relationship between quantitative and qualitative research. One view is the purest view. In the purist view of research, the two types of research represent very different paradigms that are not compatible with each other. The paradigms are so different that they cannot be combined. Purists on both sides of the research divide will often argue that one needs to stick to their preferred method. It is not uncommon to hear one side dismissing or putting down the other side as not being adequate research. The qualitative purist may say that quantitative research is so caught up in procedures and hypothesis testing, that it overlooks important findings. Because of the extreme focus on research procedures, the research results lose relevance. The quantitative purist may say that qualitative research is lacking in discipline and procedures. Because of the lack of specific proven procedures, the research conclusions cannot be trusted, and therefore, qualitative research is not a valid form of research.

The other view toward qualitative and quantitative research is sometimes called the pragmatic view. The pragmatist views the two methods as different tools that can be used either separately or together depending on the particular situation. The pragmatist would say that the researcher should use whatever works best based on the situation or to combine aspects of both approaches. Then the researcher can take advantage of the best of both worlds. It should be understood that neither the purist nor the pragmatic philosophical positions can be demonstrated to be absolutely true or false. It is the preferred position of those who have chosen sides in the debate. Each individual researcher will need to determine his or her own approach to this issue.

Based on the pragmatic view of qualitative research a new paradigm of research has recently developed. This paradigm is sometimes referred to as mixed methods research. Mixed methods research is focused on creating a research design that is partly qualitative and partly quantitative in nature. These methods may be blended or they may be separate parts of the same research study. The mixed methods approach to research has become a much more common approach to research today than in the past.

To sum up qualitative research, there are certain methods that tend to be used frequently. First of all methods are not as well developed in qualitative research as in quantitative research. Part of this reason is that less emphasis is placed on methods and more on the theory and philosophy that guide the researchers approach to conducting qualitative research. Another reason for the lack of development of specific methods is because qualitative research as a separate paradigm does not have the historical development that quantitative research has.

Although qualitative research by its very name indicates the use of words and not numbers, this does not mean that qualitative researchers never use any quantitative analysis in their research. Often qualitative researchers will use descriptive statistics in their analysis to summarize the findings that they have obtained from the qualitative analysis of their data. Qualitative research has become a common approach to conducting research. As an educational leader, having a general understanding of both qualitative and quantitative methods will be very valuable in analyzing data to make effective decisions as a leader.

CHAPTER 10

Analysis of Data

This chapter on data analysis will be a very brief, general overview of data analysis. It is beyond the scope of this text to focus on data analysis to the point that it is required to become a skilled analyst. There are many references to statistics in education and the social sciences that the reader may refer to that can explain concepts of data analysis. This chapter will be limited to a very brief and general overview of data analysis and will be focused on the needs of the educational leader to analyze data to make decisions.

The main requirement in analyzing data is to always keep the focus on the purpose and the research questions of the study. It is very easy, especially with the statistical software available today, to get lost in an over analysis of data and lose the focus of what the purpose of the analysis is. Sometimes researchers with a modest knowledge of statistics will conduct a series of statistical analyses more for the purpose of showing that they can, than for the purpose of answering the specific questions. Therefore the researcher should keep in mind the specific questions that need to be answered as the analysis proceeds.

1   Categories of Data

The next thing that the researcher needs to keep in mind is the type of data that is being analyzed. Sometimes data are in discrete categories such as gender, socioeconomic status, or racial/ethnic status. For these types of data the analysis is limited to counting the occurrence or computing the percent of occurrences in a particular category. Other types of data may be in a more continuous form referred to as interval level data. Interval level data means that data are in a rank order but also that the distance between one number and the next number is the same as between any other number and the next number. For example, the difference between a two and a three is the same as between a four and a five. If this is the case with data, there are many more options for data analysis. A third distinction of data may be that data are rank ordered but are not interval. This allows for more analysis than for categorical data but is more restricted than for interval types of data. The main thing to keep in mind is that the type of data needs to drive the analysis, not the other way around.

2 Types of Data Analysis

As stated earlier, the researcher must focus on the specific research questions that are to be answered as well as the type of data that is present. The great majority of data analysis that is necessary for making educational decisions can be referred to as descriptive statistics. In descriptive statistics frequency distributions, charts, and graphs are constructed to give a visual display to interpret the data. The frequency distribution is simply a tally of the results by categories. For example the researcher may want to know the distribution of students in a class by gender. The researcher would then construct a frequency distribution tallying the number or percent of males and females in the class. To make an attractive visual display the researcher may also construct a graph of the distribution. There are many types of graphs that a researcher can use. The researcher should focus on using one that will give the best picture or representation of the data.

If the data being analyzed are interval level data, more descriptive statistics can be used to analyze the data. These include measures of central tendency, variability, and relationships. Central tendency can be broken down into three different statistics, the mean, median, and mode. The mean is the most commonly used measure of central tendency. It is what we generally think of as being an average. It is sometimes referred to as the arithmetical average of data. To compute the average, the researcher adds up the total of all of the numbers and divides by the number of cases that are analyzed.

Often data will form a pattern that is referred to as a normal curve. In a normal curve the data are shaped much like a bell and is sometimes referred to as a bell-shaped curve. This distribution of data is also symmetrical in that most of the data are in the middle of the range of data and fewer and fewer instances of the data are found the further one goes from the middle of the distribution. In a symmetrical distribution, the data are similar on both sides of the distribution. In fact, in a perfect normal curve, the distribution would be the same on both sides. If this is the case the mean is the most valuable statistic to use for analysis. However, sometimes data do not form a normal distribution and the data are skewed in one direction or another. If data are skewed this means that the data tend to bunch up on one side of the distribution or the other. In this case the mean of the data will also be skewed and may lead to a misleading interpretation of the data. For these types of data the median is often used to represent the midpoint or central tendency of data. The median is the midpoint of the data where 50% of the data is above the median and 50% of the data is below the median. The median is not as affected by extreme scores in the distribution as the mean.

If data are categorical in nature the only measure of central tendency that is appropriate is the mode. The mode is simply the most frequently occurring value in a distribution. However, except for categorical types of data, the mode is not the most useful measure of central tendency.

While the central tendency is very important to understand the distribution of data, it is only one concept that is useful in understanding data. The next type of data representation is the variability of data. It is often important that the researcher understand not only the central tendency of data but also the variability of the data. As educators we have an intuitive understanding of the importance of variability in a distribution. Sometimes we have a class that is very homogeneous and all of the students tend to be somewhat similar in ability and achievement. Other times we may have a class that is much more diverse in ability and achievement levels. This type of class is referred to as a heterogeneous class. Although the two classes may have the same average level of achievement, they are very different in the variability of ability and the teacher would need to approach the two classes differently. Without the use of any statistics we have demonstrated the importance of understanding variability in a distribution of data.

Variability of data can be measured in several ways including the range, interquartile range, and standard deviation. The type of variability we use depends largely on the type of data that we have. If we have categorical data the only measure of variability that we can use is the range or the difference between the highest and lowest category. If our data are rank-ordered, we can use what is referred to as an interquartile range. The interquartile range is a range between the first quartile and the fourth quartile, or the middle 50% of the distribution. This statistic gives an indication of how the middle half of the distribution is spread out and is not affected by extreme outlier scores. One chart that is often used today and is easily constructed with statistical software programs is called the box and whisker plot. The box and whisker plot represents the range and the interquartile range of a set of data. The box is constructed that represents the interquartile range or the range between the 25th percentile and the 75th percentile of the data. The box is divided in two at the median of the data. The whiskers or lines then extend out for the entire range of the data on both sides. The box and whisker chart makes a good visual representation of how data are spread out in a distribution. See Figure 10.1 for an example of a box and whisker plot of a distribution of data in a hypothetical classroom.

The final way of representing the variability of data is the use of the standard deviation. The mathematics behind the standard deviation are complex and beyond the scope of this text. It is the most frequently used

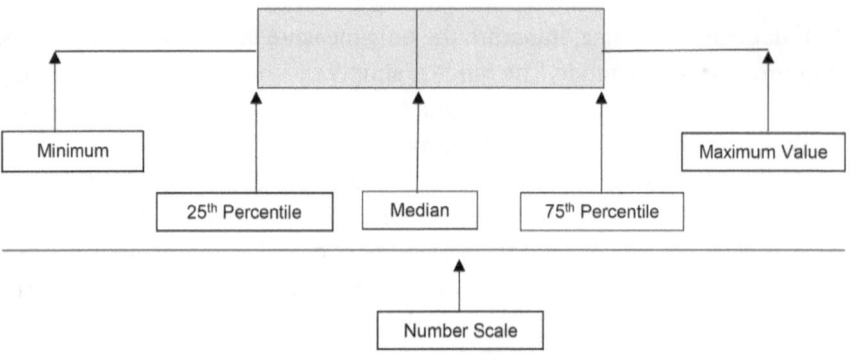

FIGURE 10.1   *Data representation in a box and whisker plot*

measure of variability in statistics and is the basis from which most statistical inference procedures are derived. In concept the standard deviation can be used to determine the variation of the distribution in precise numbers. In a normal distribution it is very predictable how many cases in a distribution will vary around a certain distance from the mean. This statistic is also the basis of many types of scores in psychology and educational measurement. These are referred to as standard scores. Standard scores are based on a mean and a standard deviation. Some standard scores that are often used that are based on the mean and standard deviation of data, are Z scores, T scores, SAT scores, ACT scores, GRE scores and many others. The main idea to remember is that the use of a statistic such as the mean and standard deviation are the basis for many psychological and educational measurements as well as for inferential statistics. Again many statistics textbooks and resource books will give a thorough treatment of these topics.

For the educational leader, having a good understanding of basic descriptive statistics is important. This understanding will be very valuable and provide useful tools for analyzing data at a classroom, school, or district level to make effective decisions.

Another branch of statistics that is well beyond the scope of this text is referred to as inferential statistics. Inferential statistics go beyond just describing a set of data that may be of interest to the educational leader. Most decisions in a classroom or school can be made with a good analysis of descriptive statistics. Researchers though are often interested in understanding not just data from a particular setting but in drawing inferences to a larger population. This is the case in most research. In this case the researcher would be much more interested in inferential statistics so that the researcher can draw inferences beyond a particular study and to a larger population. This is referred to as generalizability in research or external validity. These concepts were discussed earlier and are very important for the educational researcher who is interested mostly in publishing research results in academic journals or in professional conferences. However this is not the scope of this text and the reader is referred to many quality statistical textbooks.

After analyzing data, the educational leader needs to interpret what the results mean. This interpretation should refer back to the research questions that are driving the analysis. The leader then should ask himself what the results of the analysis mean for further decision-making. The leader must also be careful not to over-interpret the data and to stay within the scope of the data that were analyzed. There is often a temptation to over interpret results and to make decisions beyond what is supported by the data analysis. One common example of this is when a small change occurs in results major decisions are made based on the small results. Over interpreting results of analysis can lead to poor decisions and sometimes may be as bad as no analysis at all. It is very useful to analyze data to help make decisions, but it is also important that the analysis of data is not over interpreted beyond what is appropriate for that particular situation.

In conclusion, analysis of data needs to take place in any research study in order to make conclusions about the study. After the analysis of data is conducted the conclusions from the analysis then form the basis for decisions to improve practices in the school or classroom.

CHAPTER 11

Research Results
Conclusions, Decisions, and Actions

This chapter will focus on the conclusions, decisions, and actions from a research report. Research reports normally need to be in a written format and hints will be given about good reporting practices for research reports. The educational leader needs to keep in mind the audience for a report as well as the sophistication of the audience. The main requirement in any good research report is that it communicates effectively with its audience. If one is communicating to a faculty meeting, the person must realize that these are professional teachers with a lot of knowledge of their profession and their situation. However they do not generally have a lot of technical knowledge about research. If the report is going to the school board the researcher needs to be aware that the school board consists of laypeople who generally do not have a high technical knowledge but are knowledgeable of the policy responsibilities of school board members. Whatever the audience, it is important to keep in mind how best to communicate with that audience.

1 Sections of a Research Report

In a formal research report there is an introduction that describes the study. The introduction would comprise Chapter 1 of a dissertation. After the introduction there is usually a problem statement or a justification for the research. After the problem statement, a purpose statement shortly describes the purpose for conducting the research. Next, research questions or hypotheses are generally stated that are addressed in the research project. The introduction usually concludes with a statement of what will be accomplished through the research project. In a dissertation these topics are expanded into the first chapter of the dissertation and include other topics in addition to those outlined here. In a professional research journal article these topics are addressed but usually in a more succinct manner. In a report to a school audience this may be done in a very informal way but still the researcher needs to orient the audience to the research project.

In a dissertation, chapter 2 consists of a review of the literature. In a journal article, a review of the literature is also conducted but will vary in length depending on the type of research and journal article in which it is published.

The literature is a summary of previous work that is been related to the study. The literature review will demonstrate a familiarity with previous research and how that relates to the planned study. It is important in the literature review to demonstrate how the previous literature supports the importance of the study and the need for the study. The literature review should be related to the planned study and support it. However in a school or district level research report, the literature review may be left out and only the introduction and background used to document the reasons for the study.

Chapter 3 in a dissertation shows the procedures that were used in conducting the study. The procedures should address the population and sample if there was a sample and how the sample was obtained. Instrumentation or the measurement of variables should be addressed. This will describe which variables were used in the study and how they were measured. It is critically important that the instruments measure the variables accurately and with validity. If the variables are not measured accurately, the data collected will probably lead to disappointing results and perhaps to useless results. The variables need to be measured not only accurately but accurately for the purposes of the research. For example it may be tempting to use a test or some other instrument as the measurement tool in a project. However, if the measurement tool is not aligned with the variables being measured, false or invalid measurement will result.

After the instrumentation section, the research design should be described. The research design is the type of research that was discussed earlier in Chapter 8. The next step is to describe the procedural detail about how the study was conducted. This should be a detailed step-by-step discussion that the researcher used in conducting the study and collecting data. Any threats to internal validity should also be addressed in the procedures. Finally a data analysis plan is presented describing how the data were analyzed after they were collected.

These procedures make up chapter 3 in a dissertation and are also described in a journal article but generally not in as much detail as in a dissertation. It is still important that the reader understand how the research was conducted so that the study could be replicated if desired. For a school level report this section may be very informal and short. However the audience should still be oriented to how the study was conducted and how the data were obtained for the study.

Chapter 4 in a dissertation is where the results of the study are reported. This chapter is limited to the reporting of the results without an interpretation of their meaning or implications for the results. The analyses should be described and a description of any statistical analyses should be included in this section.

Next the results of the statistical or qualitative analyses are reported and summarized. After the results are reported in the conclusions are made about what the analysis meant.

In a professional journal article this may be the heart of the article. This section provides all of the results from the analysis of data for the study. In a school level report this is also a very important section, but the researcher needs to keep in mind the sophistication and interests of the audience. This section tells the audience what was discovered and what was learned through the analysis of the data. This is a very important section whether it is in a dissertation, a journal article, or a school report. The only difference will be in the formality in which the results are presented and in the length in which they are presented.

Regardless of the formality of the report, it is important the researcher stays within the data in interpreting the results. The researcher should be careful not to overgeneralize conclusions or to make conclusions that are not directly supported by the analysis of the data. Overgeneralizing results can mislead the audience into ascribing more importance to the findings than is justified. It also is an indication of bias by the researcher who may be viewing his or her work more highly than it deserves to be viewed. For the educational leader, this overstatement can lead to a loss of credibility if stakeholders see through the overstatements.

The last chapter in a dissertation, Chapter 5, provides a summary of the research and the implications of the results. The implications for theory and for practice are described and the results are placed in a broader context beyond the study itself. The results are related back to the literature and a description is made about how the results enhance the literature on the subject that was studied. Limitations of the study are also stated or perhaps restated. Based on the results that were presented in chapter 4 recommendations for further research are often included. This section of the report allows more freedom for the researcher to expand beyond the strict conclusions of the study into the implication of the study for further research and practice.

In a journal article this section concludes the article with a summary of the results of the study and the meaning that the results have in the context of the study. This summary also provides recommendations for further research in the field and how the research can be expanded in this particular topic. The only difference with the dissertation is that the article will be much shorter on this topic than the entire chapter of a dissertation.

In a school level report this section is also very important and may be the most important part of the research report. Often an audience such as a school board may not be very interested in the technical details of how the results were obtained, but very interested in what the results mean and the implications of the results. This is where the results are put into the context and conclusions are made about what next steps may be indicated. The section may also include a plan of action of steps that will be taken based on the analysis of data that will lead to improvement in the particular situation that is being studied.

2   Writing the Research Report

When writing a research report, there are several general rules that the researcher should consider and follow. The first major rule as mentioned above is to understand the audience for the presentation. The researcher should consider the sophistication, technical level, and interest level of the audience. The presentation needs to be tailored to the sophistication, level, and the interest of the audience. If the presentation is over the heads of the audience members, they will probably not understand it and may even resent the presenter. This will create barriers to making needed changes. Moreover if the interest level of members is marginal, they will soon get bored with the presentation and tune out the presenter. In either case, the audience will only receive the report favourably if the researcher communicates with them on an appropriate level and engaging manner.

If the presentation is being presented at a faculty meeting or a team meeting, the presentation may be rather informal. Faculty members will have an understanding of the instructional implications of the report but will probably not have much of an understanding about the research procedures used. If the presentation is to the school board, a greater level of formality is generally required but the researcher needs to keep in mind the technical sophistication or lack of it of the board members. Whether it is a school board, faculty meeting, or a department meeting of specialists in a particular subject area, the researcher will be wise to understand the audience and tailor the presentation to that audience.

Underlying all of these techniques of presentation is a major concept for the leader, effective communication. If the researcher or leader is not effectively communicating with the audience, then the audience will not understand the report and will not embrace it. It is best to remember that communication is a process and usually goes beyond a single event, like a meeting. Communication is enhanced by using both verbal and written communication of results. The presentations whether written or oral should be geared to be understandable to the audience. The researcher should encourage two-way communication in discussing results. This two way communication should enhance the ability of the audience to accept and act on the results of the study.

There are several general rules of writing to consider. The first one is to write clearly and concisely. For most school situations, it is best to avoid the highly technical language of professional journals and communicate on a level that is engaging for the audience. The audience in a school situation is generally going to be very busy and will not want to have to read through a lot of verbose unnecessary writing. Writing a research report also requires good technical writing skills so that the reporting of the data is straightforward and easy to understand for the audience. Examples are often very helpful in explain a concept to an audience. Writing a research report to an audience is a skill in itself and is a different type of writing than is often done for other purposes in education.

Another important point is to avoid jargon. Simple direct language is much preferred. Every discipline and especially education has its own set of technical vocabulary that is usually understood only by those in the profession. In addition terms are often used that are specific to a particular level of education or sometimes particular to school district or school. The writer has to be conscious of the background experiences of the audience and use language that is easily understood and not jargon-type language that is only understood within a certain context. The researcher should try to avoid using many references or footnotes. This can distract from the readability of the report. Finally, even though research reports by their nature are usually rather dry reports, the presenter should strive to make the writing as interesting and understandable as possible.

Formal research reports are always written in the past tense. The past tense is used because they analysis on the results took place in the past. Formal reports such as dissertations or journal articles need to use the particular writing style as specified by the journal or the university. In education publications, the APA style is generally used. Universities often have additional requirements that need to be addresses. The researcher should be very careful to follow whatever requirements that the journal or university or other agency requires for that particular publication.

Finally it is a very good practice to have an outside editor review the report and make corrections and changes. The writer, no matter how skilled and competent, can easily miss certain things that seem very clear to the writer but are not clear to the reader. A good outside editor can also be very helpful to catch silly mistakes that can detract from the overall quality and credibility of the report. It can be very embarrassing for a leader to be presenting to the faculty and have a misspelled word or grammatical mistakes in the body of the report. This can easily be avoided by editing the work carefully and then having an outside editor go over and check the report and proofread the report. The researcher wants to be sure that there is nothing that detracts from the main message that is being presented from the research study.

3   Presenting Results of a Research Study

When the educational leader is planning a presentation of research that is being conducted, the reporting itself needs to also be well-planned. Timelines are often very important in reporting results. Sometimes decisions have to be made at a certain time of year and the reporting of the results needs to take place before those decisions need to be made. This requirement will guide the entire conduct of the research study and especially reporting timelines.

There are several ways in which the researcher can work within time limitations. Depending on the situations, reports may be delivered at regularly scheduled meetings that fall within the time constraints of the project. Sometimes results may need to be presented at impromptu meetings or a series of meetings to cover all the stakeholders. Progress or interim reports are also used to keep stakeholders informed about the progress being made, especially if it is a long term project. This will also act to prepare them as the project progresses for the results that will come.

The types of reports are also very important to consider. We often think of reports as being formal, written documents. While this is the most common form of reporting of research, other forms of reporting should also be considered. Again the researcher should consider the type of audience that will receive the report and how best to communicate with his audience. Sometimes static paper presentations are the most important. Sometimes there is a need to make an oral presentation summarizing the results. Often the educational leader will find that both methods are necessary.

The results from a research study may be somewhat sensitive or controversial to an audience. The educational leader needs to be aware of the sensitivities and possible controversies in the report and prepare for them in advance. The researcher needs to address the sensitive information in the most appropriate way and cannot hide the information. The researcher needs to be careful with this information and present it in a way that increases the likelihood that it will be accepted. The researcher should think about the context of presenting the information. Perhaps the information should only be shared with a select few individuals who have a need to know it or will need to act on it. This information is perhaps best shared verbally at first before the final report is completed.

4   Key Factors in Presenting Research

The main factors to consider for the researcher are accuracy, balance, and fairness. It is absolutely essential that the report is accurate in all of its facts and conclusions. Nothing will destroy the credibility of report faster than to find mistakes and inaccuracies in the report.

The second factor to consider is balance. Sometimes research reports are controversial or they may bring bad news that requires serious action. The audience may not be aware of or may not be prepared to deal with the topic. This can cause resistance to accepting the results if the researcher is not careful in presenting the results. The researcher needs to be sensitive to the audience and tailor the results to the audience. The researcher cannot hide the negative information, but must find a way to report it in a way that maximizes the chances of it being accepted by the audience. Almost all programs have their strengths and weaknesses. One tactic that the researcher can use is to highlight some of the strengths that were found in the situation that was being studied. By highlighting some of the strengths that are involved, it may make the negative results more acceptable to the audience. The audience has to accept the results of the findings before they will commit to actions for improvement.

The next topic that is absolutely critical for the researcher is that the reporting of the results is fair and lacking in bias. If the audience perceives the researcher to be biased in the conclusions, the audience will almost always reject the findings of the report and will either criticize the report or find a way to ignore the results. One way to maintain fairness is to closely stay within the data. By staying within the data the researcher can easily document the basis for any conclusions that were made. Staying within the data also protects the researcher from accusations of imbalance, bias, or lack of fairness.

In conclusion the reports should present a professional appearance and make an impression that the report is a serious study worth reading and taking action. For a school board presentation or a journal article there may be specific requirements of format, and length that the researcher will need to address. The report should make an attractive impression and look like an engaging report to be taken seriously. This is sometimes referred to as face validity. Face validity means that the report or presentation makes a good first impression on the reader so that the reader will want to read or listen to the report.

A research report at a school or district level should lead to action. This is the primary purpose of doing research at this level; it is not for publication or theory building. Some time will always be required to explain the research and work through some of the issues that the audience may have with the report. The end goal is to move toward corrective actions or the implementation of a plan for improvement.

The process of conducting research can be somewhat daunting for the inexperienced researcher. However by following the procedures outlined in this text, the educational leader can learn to ask the right questions, follow basic procedures, and use the information obtained to make better decisions. Research at the school or district level does not need to be highly sophisticated to be effective. Following the basics of good research, the educational leader can become quite expert in using data to guide better decisions to improve the conditions of a situation and to lead the school or district to new heights.

Further Reading

Fraenkel, J. R., Wallen, N. E., & Hyun, H. H. (2015). *How to design and evaluate research in education* (9th ed.). New York, NY: McGraw Hill.

Kubiszyn, T., & Borich, G. D. (2013). *Educational testing and measurement: Classroom application and practice* (10th ed.). Hoboken, NJ: John Wiley and Sons, Inc.

Index

Action research   5, 37, 46, 47
Alternate forms reliability   28

Bias   13, 14, 16–21, 31–35, 40, 47, 48, 52, 53, 62, 66

Concurrent validity   25, 26
Construct validity   25–27
Content validity   25–27
Correlational research   6, 37, 41, 42
Criterion validity   25, 26

Data analysis   2, 8, 50, 55–59, 61
Data-based decision making   2
Descriptive research   7

Experimental research   6, 37–42, 53
External validity   21, 22, 26, 31–37, 46–48, 58

Instruction   1, 23, 40, 50, 63
Internal consistency reliability   28
Internal validity   31–38, 40–42, 45, 47, 48, 61

Measurement   8, 23–30, 58, 61

Non-random sampling   17, 20, 21

Populations   6, 8, 15–22, 37, 43, 47, 48, 51, 52, 58, 61
Predictive validity   25, 26
Problem statement   7, 9–12, 50, 60
Purpose statement   7, 9–12, 43, 50, 60

Qualitative research   6, 49–54
Quantitative research   6, 49, 50, 52–54

Random sampling   17–20, 50, 52
Reliability   23–25, 27–30, 35
Reporting results   65
Research designs   31, 36–48, 53, 54, 61
Research questions   4, 7–12, 23, 30, 49, 50, 55, 56, 59, 60
Reviewing literature   13–22

Sampling   15–22, 50–52
Scientific method   4, 5, 7, 11, 49, 50

Test-retest reliability   28
Threats to validity   31–36, 45, 47
Types of knowledge   3, 4
Types of research   5, 6, 37, 41, 43, 46, 47, 49, 53, 60, 61

Validity of measurements   25, 27–29, 61

www.ingramcontent.com/pod-product-compliance
Lightning Source LLC
LaVergne TN
LVHW042046070526
838201LV00077B/815